FOR ORGANS, PIANOS & ELECTRONIC KEYBOARDS

E-Z PLAY® TODAY

195

Opera FAVORITES

T0080185

Cover Photo: Interior View of Teatro La Fenice / Venice, Italy
Photo Credit: Cameraphoto Arte Venezia / The Bridgeman Art Library

ISBN 978-1-4803-6950-4

HAL•LEONARD®
CORPORATION

7777 W. BLUEMOUND RD. P.O. BOX 13819 MILWAUKEE, WI 53213

Visit Hal Leonard Online at
www.halleonard.com

Addio del passato
from LA TRAVIATA

Registration 3
Rhythm: Waltz

By Giuseppe Verdi

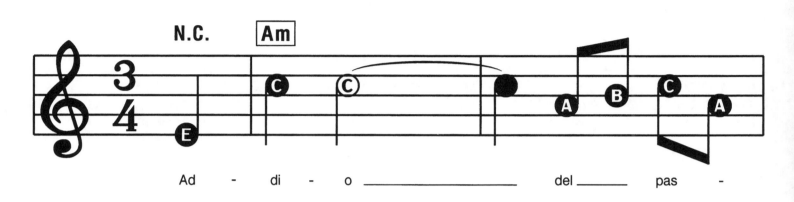

Ad - di - o _____ del _____ pas -

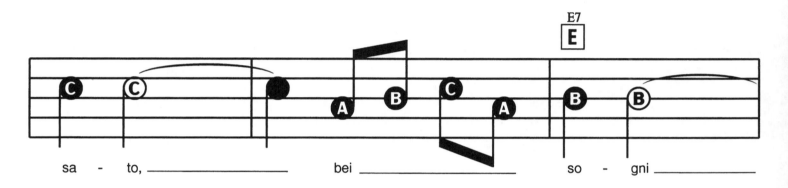

sa - to, _____ bei _____ so - gni _____

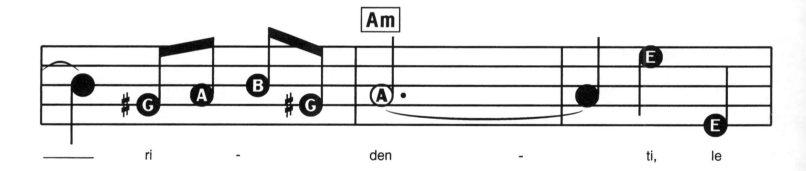

_____ ri - den _____ ti, le

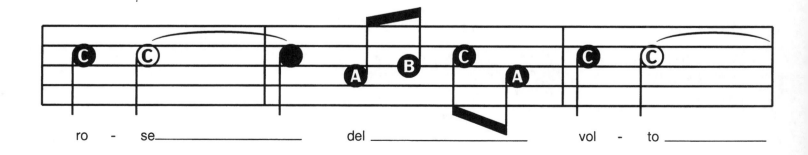

ro - se _____ del _____ vol - to _____

5

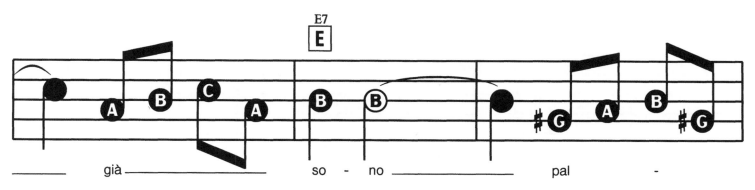

già _____ so - no _____ pal -

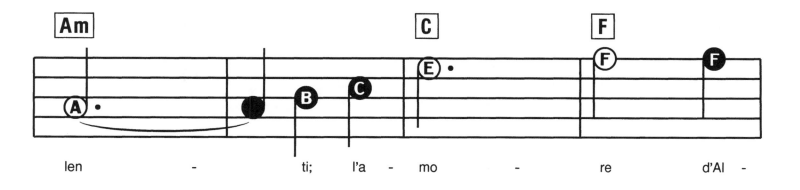

len - ti; l'a - mo - re d'Al -

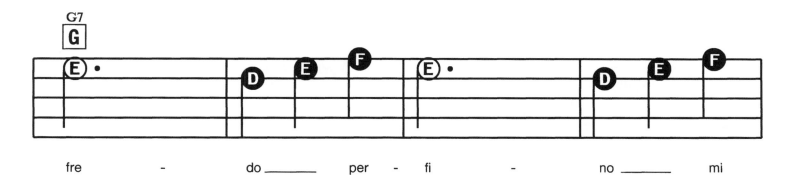

fre - do _____ per - fi - no _____ mi

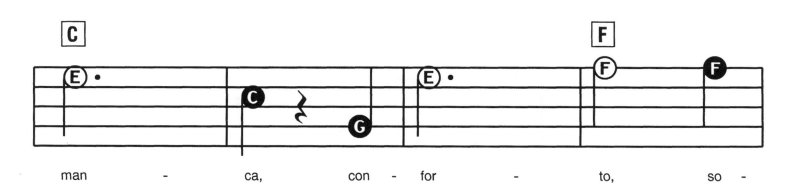

man - ca, con - for - to, so -

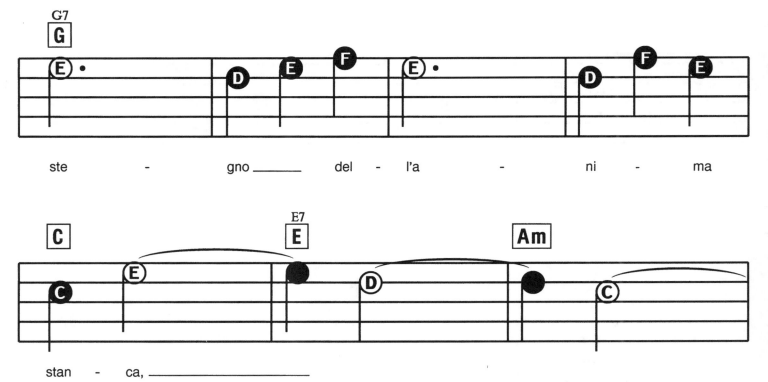

ste - gno _____ del - l'a - ni - ma

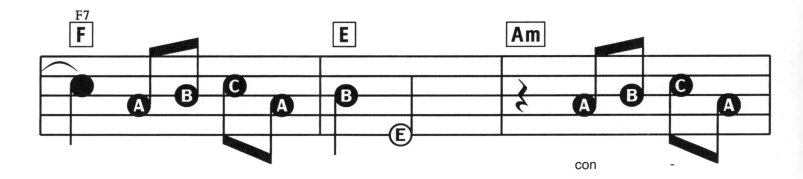

stan - ca, _____

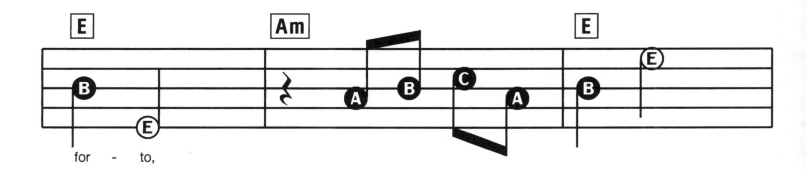

con -

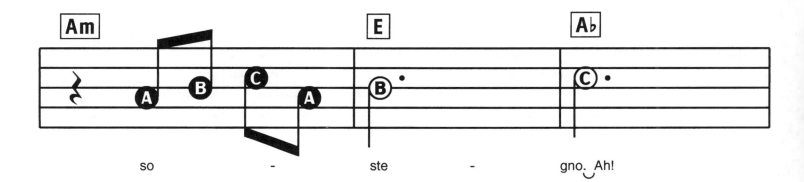

for - to,

so - ste - gno. Ah!

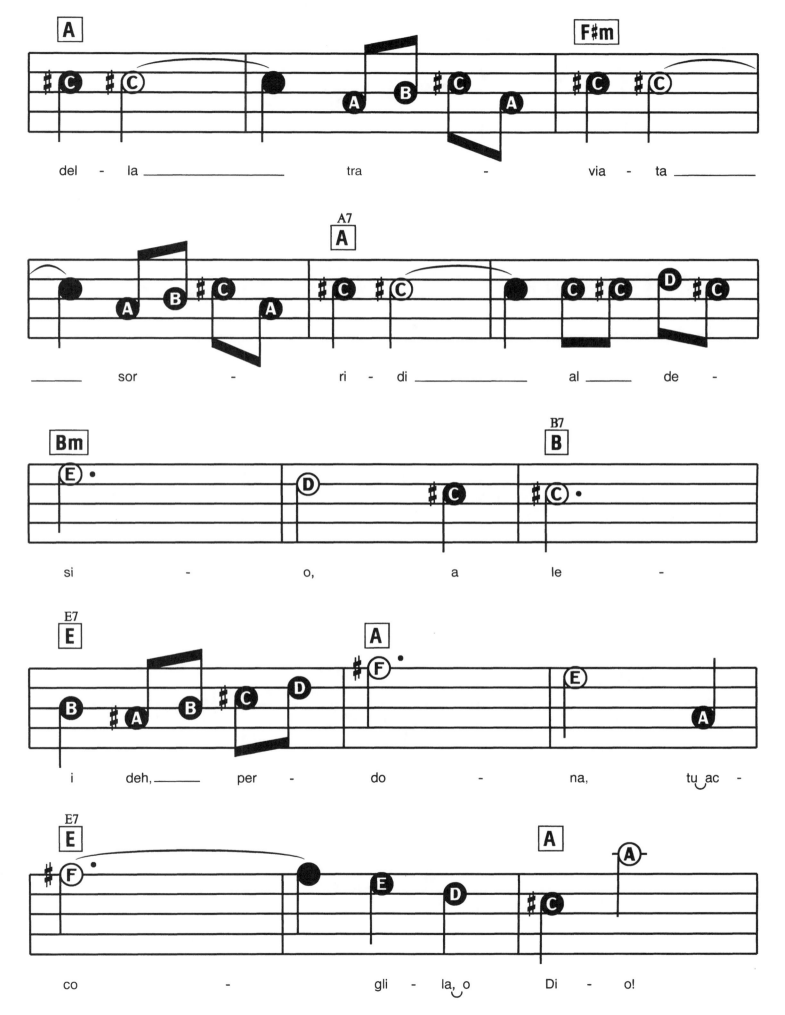

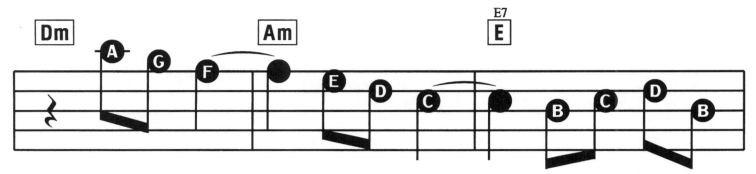

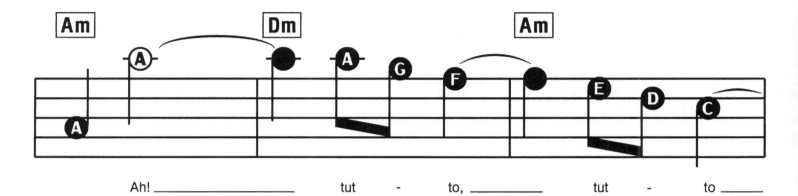

Ah! _____ tut - to, _____ tut - to _____

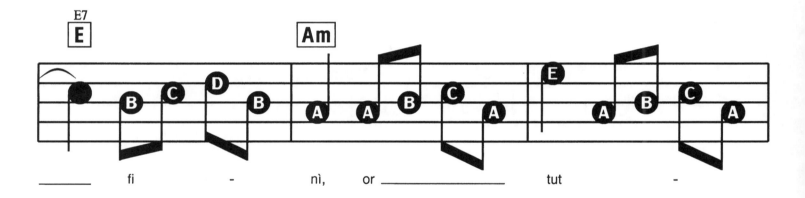

_____ fi - nì, or _____ tut -

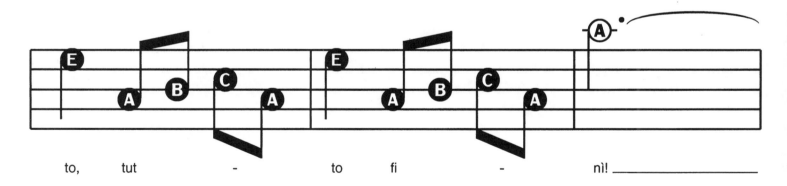

to, tut - to fi - nì! _____

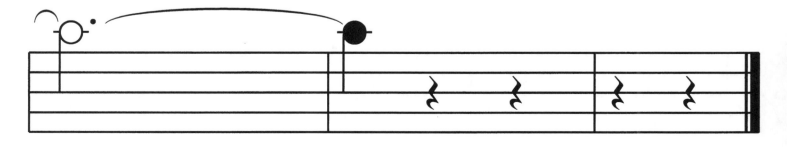

The Anvil Chorus
from IL TROVATORE

Registration 5
Rhythm: March

By Giuseppe Verdi

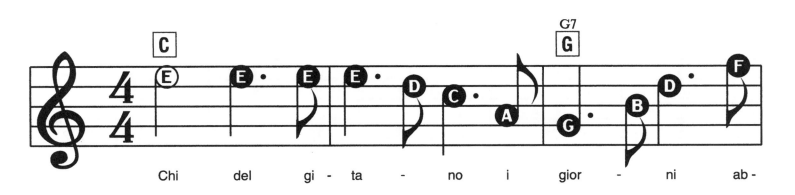

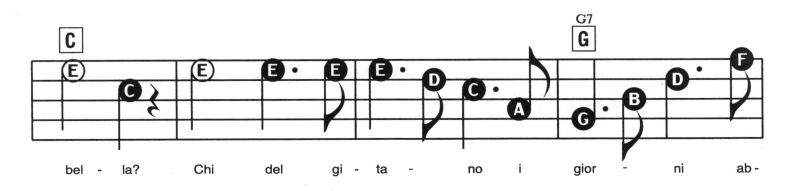

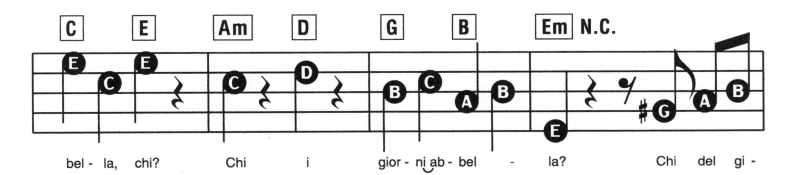

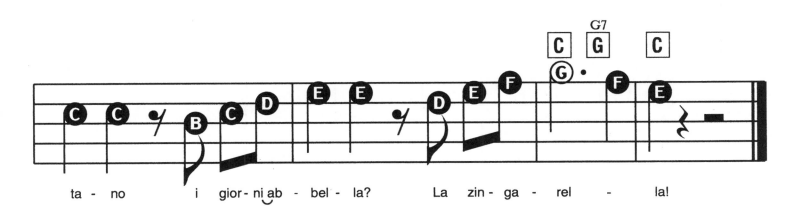

Barcarolle
from THE TALES OF HOFFMANN

Registration 1
Rhythm: Waltz

By Jacques Offenbach

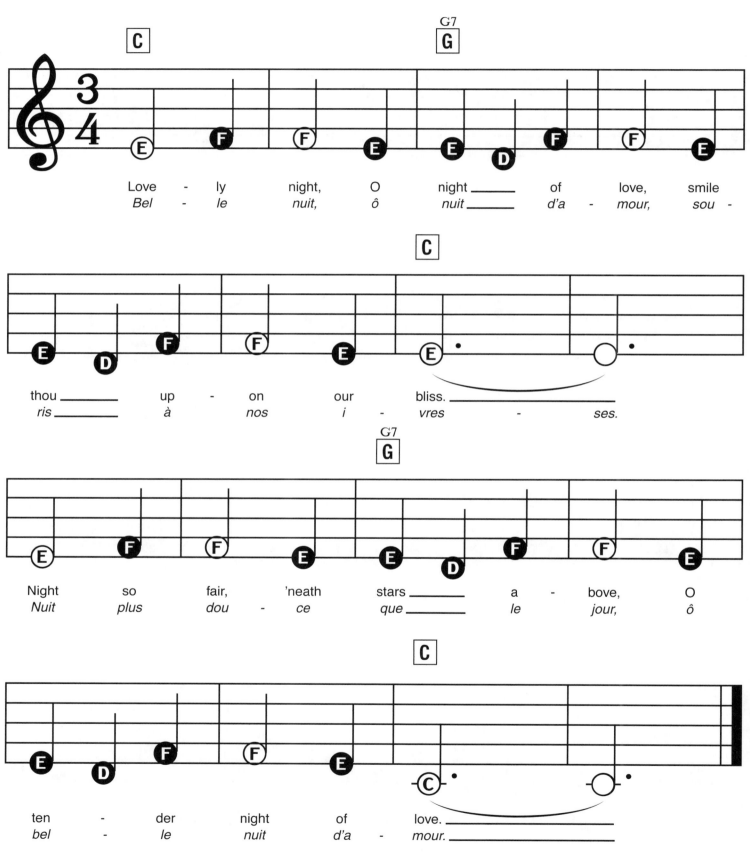

Love - ly night, O night _____ of love, smile
Bel - le nuit, ô nuit _____ d'a - mour, sou -

thou _____ up - on our bliss. _____
ris _____ à nos i - vres - ses.

Night so fair, 'neath stars _____ a - bove, O
Nuit so plus dou - ce que _____ le jour, ô

ten - der night of love. _____
bel - le nuit d'a - mour. _____

Canzone di Doretta
(Chi bel sogno di Doretta)
from LA RONDINE

Registration 8
Rhythm: Waltz or None

By Giacomo Puccini

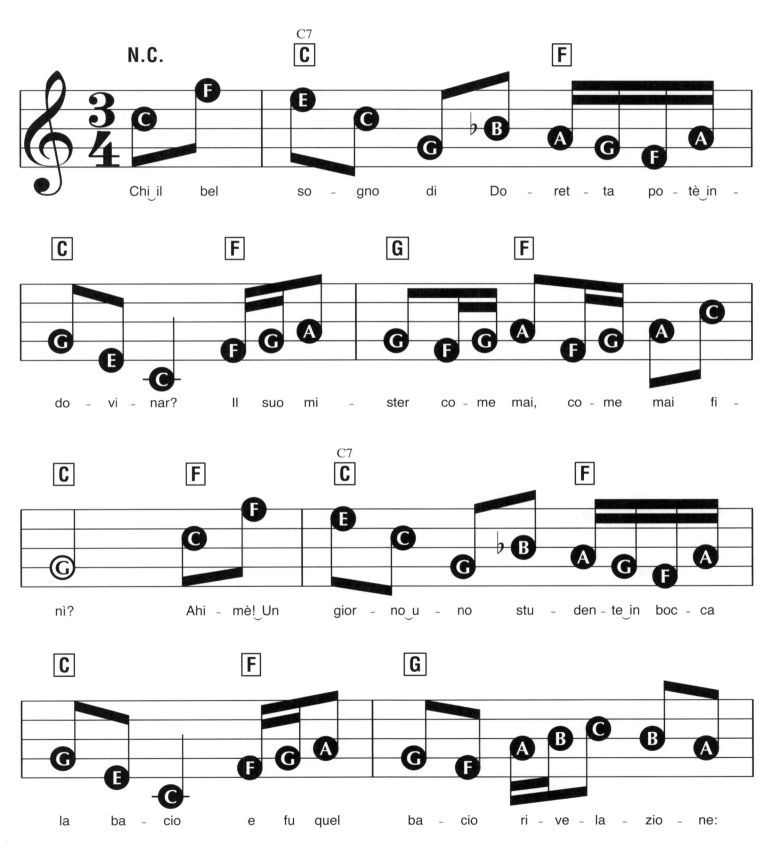

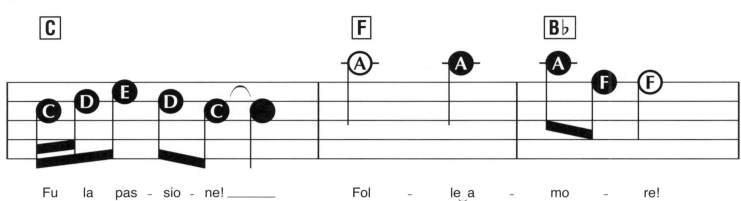

Fu la pas – sio – ne! _____ Fol – le a – mo – re!

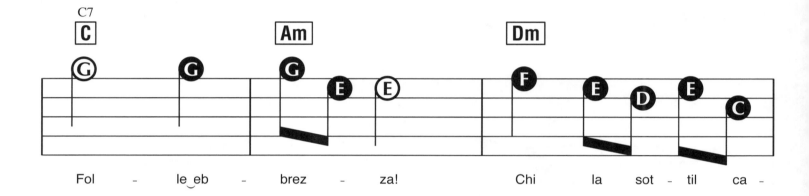

Fol – le eb – brez – za! Chi la sot – til ca –

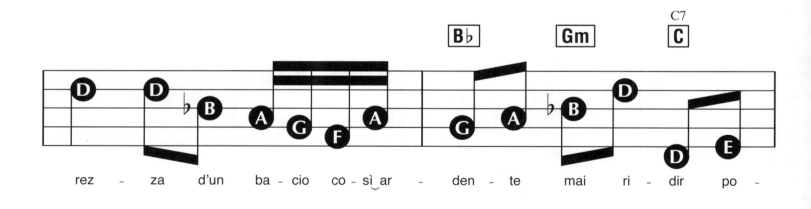

rez – za d'un ba – cio co – sì ar – den – te mai ri – dir po –

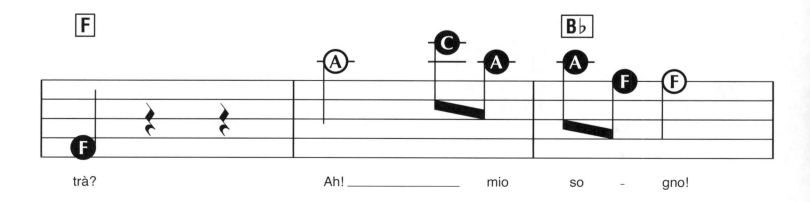

trà? Ah! _____ mio so – gno!

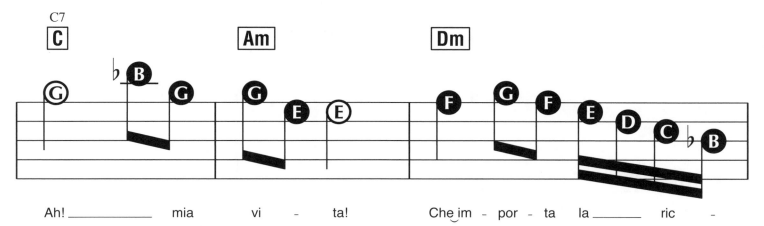

Ah! _____ mia vi - ta! Che im - por - ta la _____ ric -

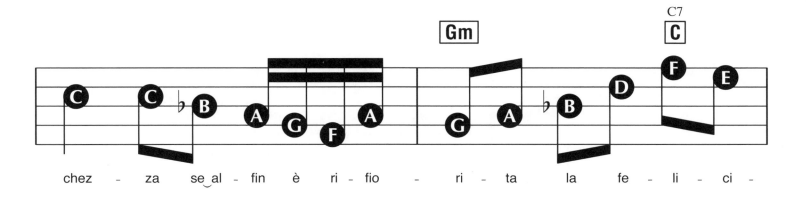

chez - za se al - fin è ri - fio - ri - ta la fe - li - ci -

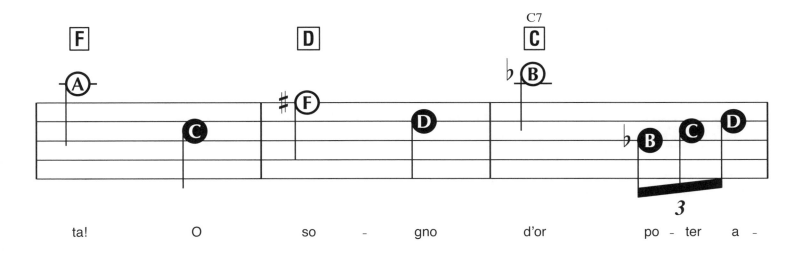

ta! O so - gno d'or po - ter a -

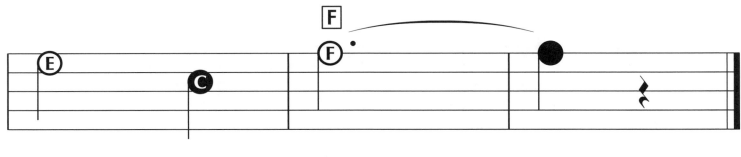

mar - co - sì! _____

Che gelida manina
from LA BOHÈME

Registration 3
Rhythm: Ballad

By Giacomo Puccini

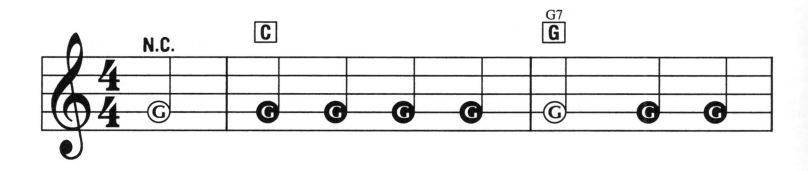

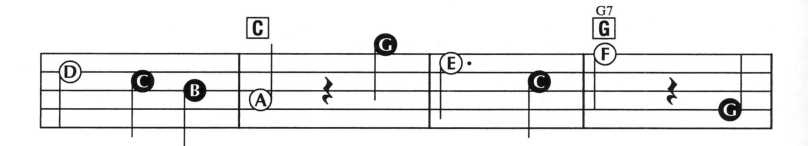

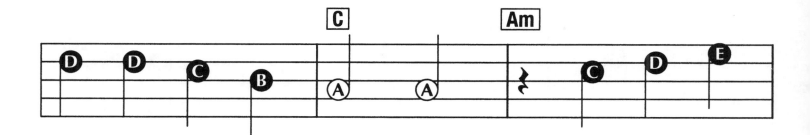

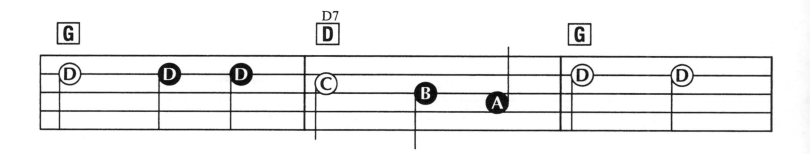

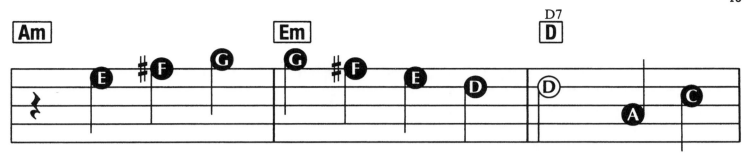

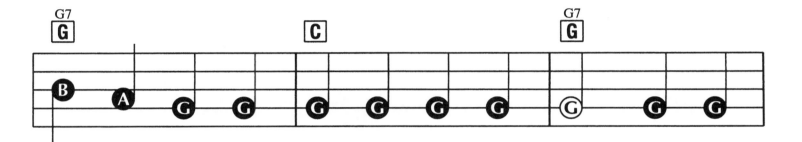

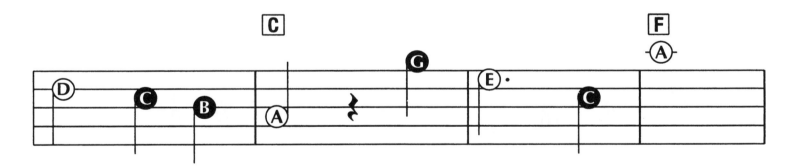

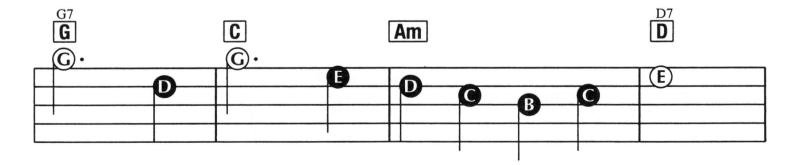

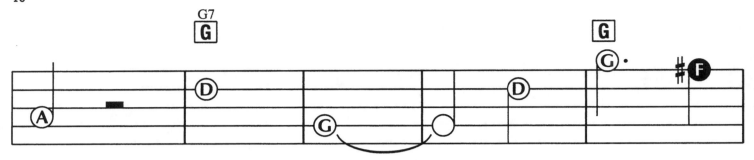

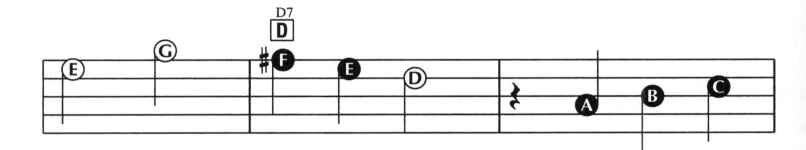

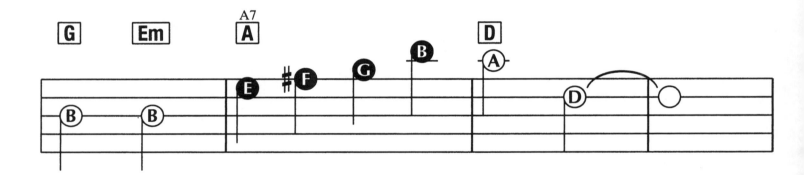

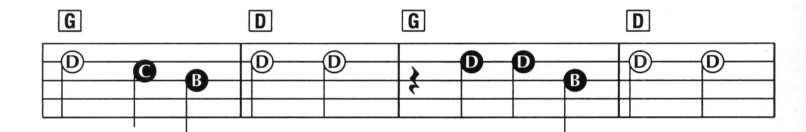

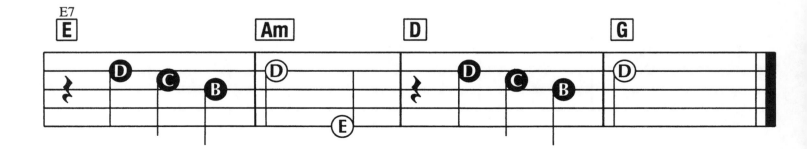

Der Vogelfänger bin ich ja
from THE MAGIC FLUTE

Registration 5
Rhythm: March or Fox Trot

Words by Emanuel Schikaneder
Music by Wolfgang Amadeus Mozart

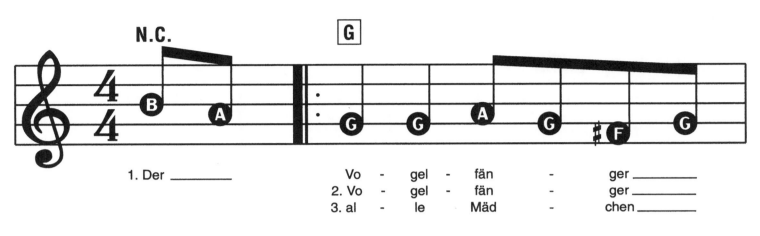

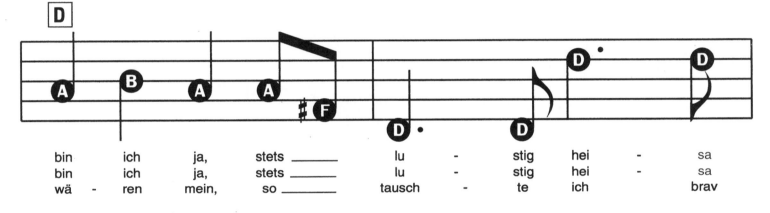

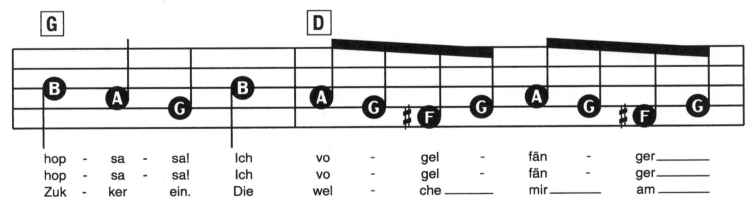

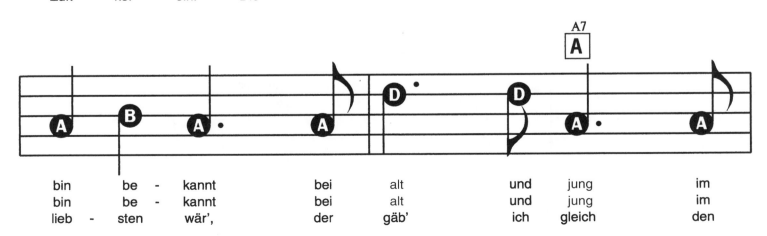

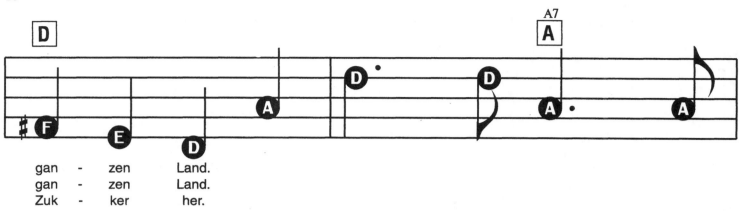

gan - zen Land.
gan - zen Land.
Zuk - ker her.

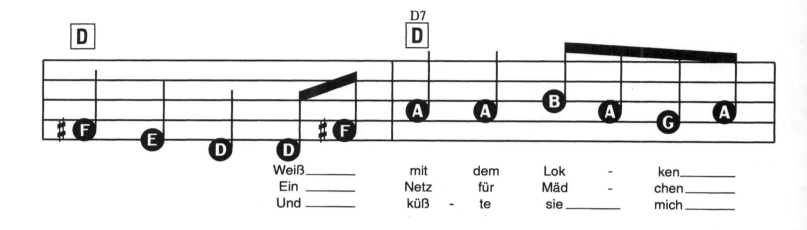

Weiß___ mit dem Lok - ken___
Ein___ Netz für Mäd - chen___
Und___ küß - te sie___ mich___

um - zu - gehn, und mich aufs Pfei - fen___
möch - te ich; und ich fing sie du - tzend -
zärt - lich dann, wär' sie mein Weib___ und___

zu ver - stehn!
weis für mich!
ich ihr Mann.

Drum _____ kann ich froh _____ und _____
Dann _____ sperr - te ich _____ sie _____
Sie _____ schleif an mei - ner _____

lu - stig sein, denn _____ al - le Vö - gel _____
bei mir ein, und _____ al - le Mäd - chen _____
Sei - te ein; ich _____ wieg - te wie _____ ein

sind ja _____ mein.
wä - ren _____ mein.
Kind sie _____ ein.

1,2

3

2. Der _____
3. Wenn _____

Contessa, perdono
from LE NOZZE DI FIGARO

Registration 1
Rhythm: 8-Beat

By Wolfgang Amadeus Mozart

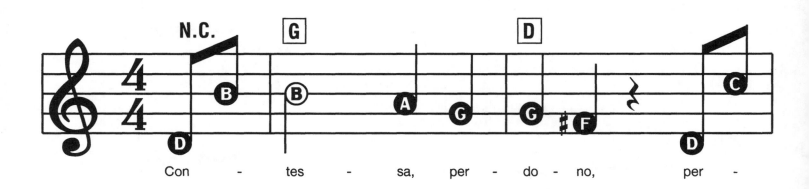

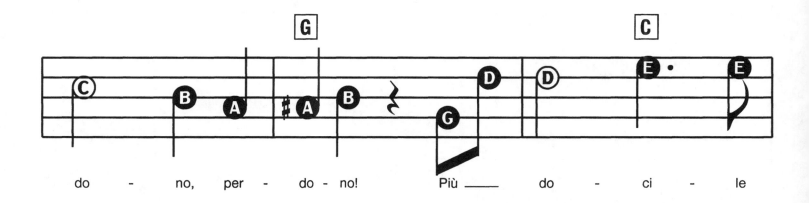

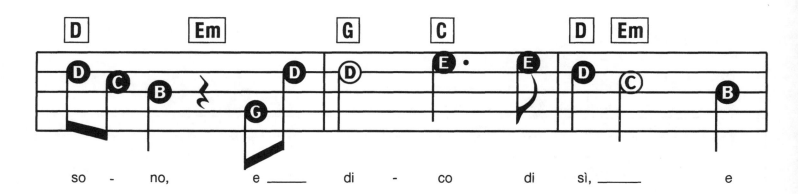

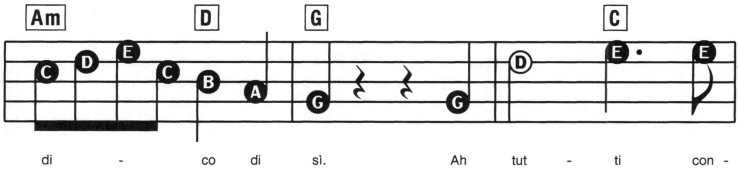

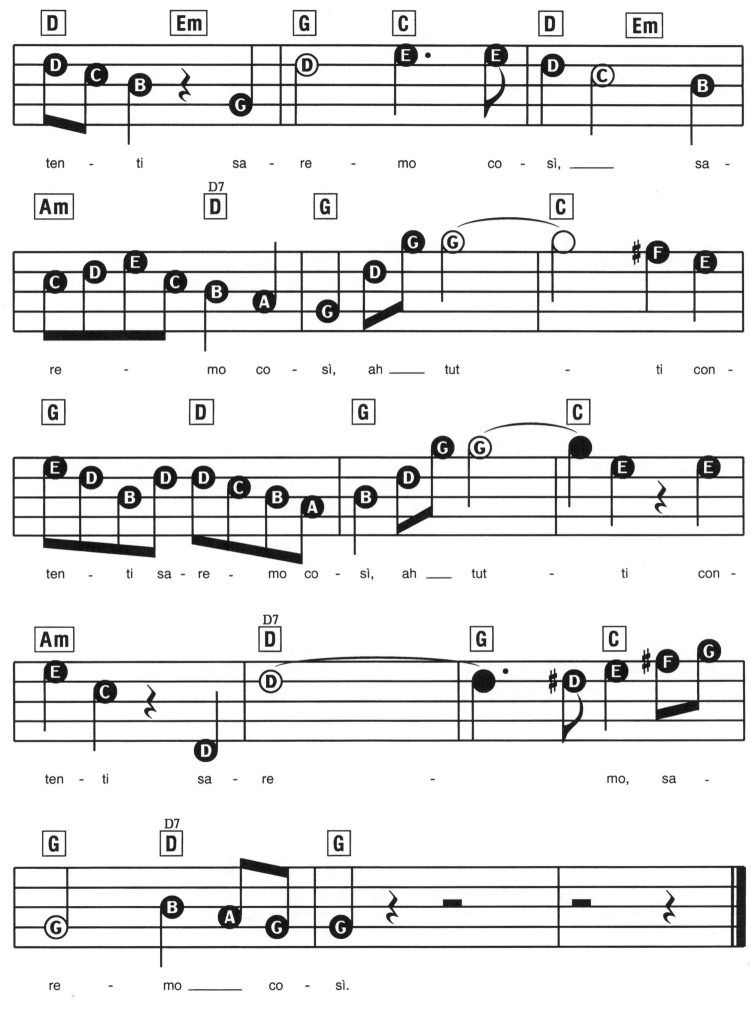

Der Hölle Rache
from THE MAGIC FLUTE

Registration 7
Rhythm: March

By Wolfgang Amadeus Mozart

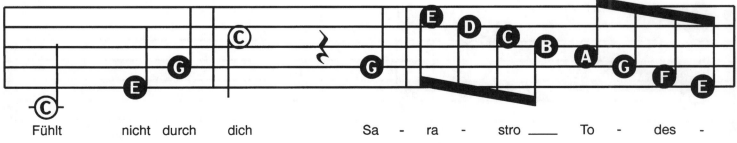

Der Höl - le   Ra - che kocht in mei - nem   Her - zen;

Tod   und Ver - zweif - lung,   Tod   und   Ver -

zweif - lung flam - men um mich   her!

Fühlt   nicht durch dich   Sa - ra - stro ___ To - des -

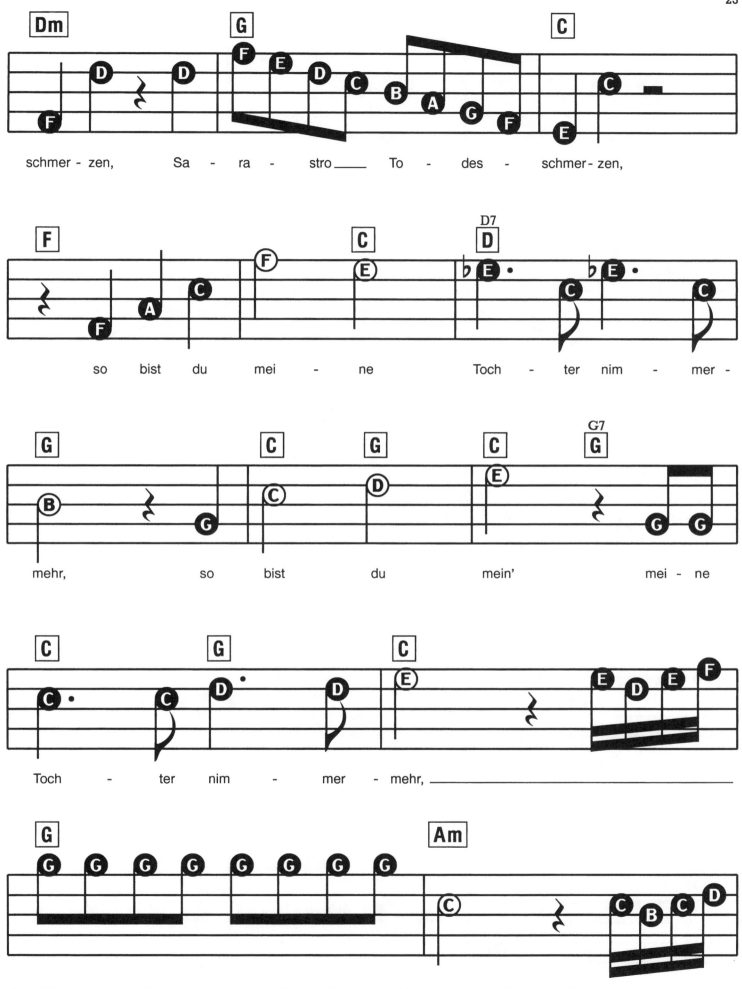

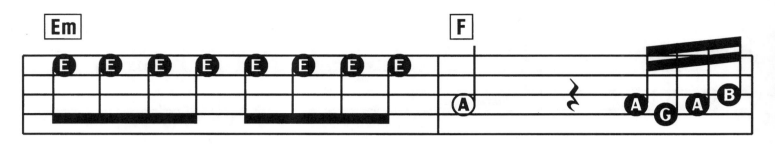

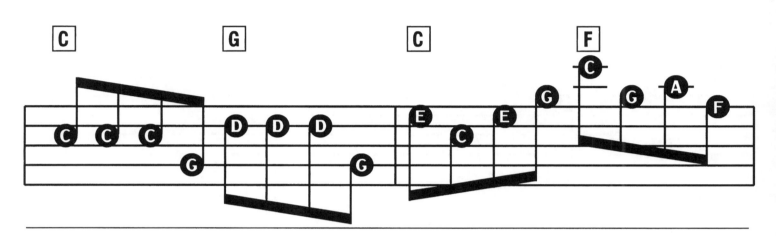

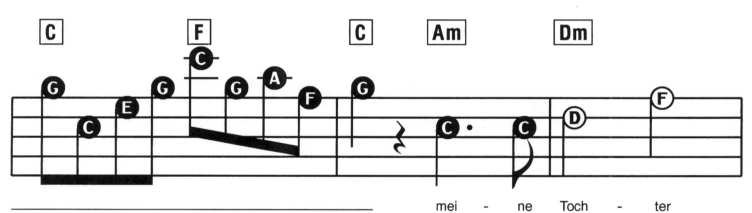

mei - ne Toch - ter

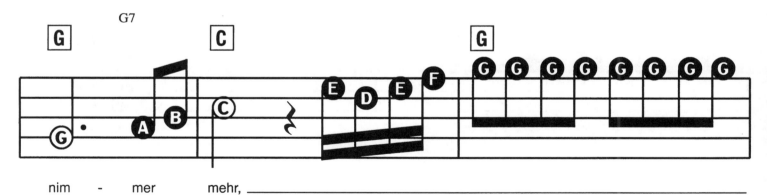

nim - mer mehr,

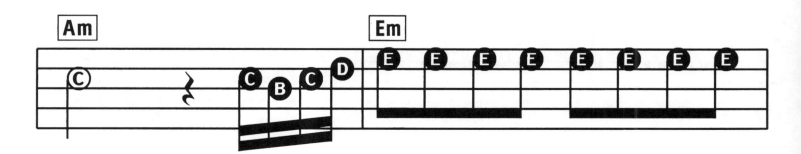

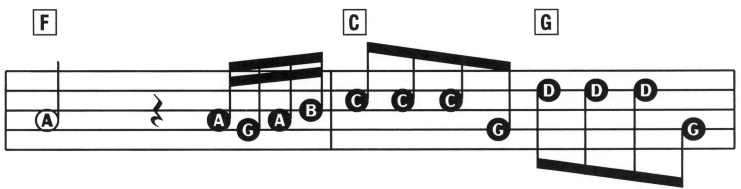

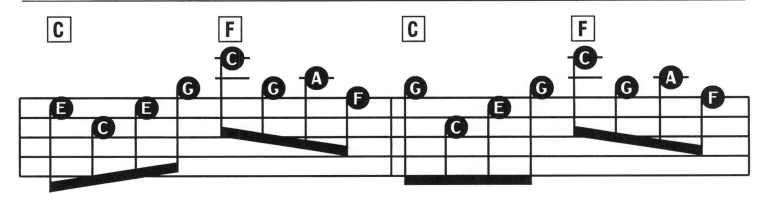

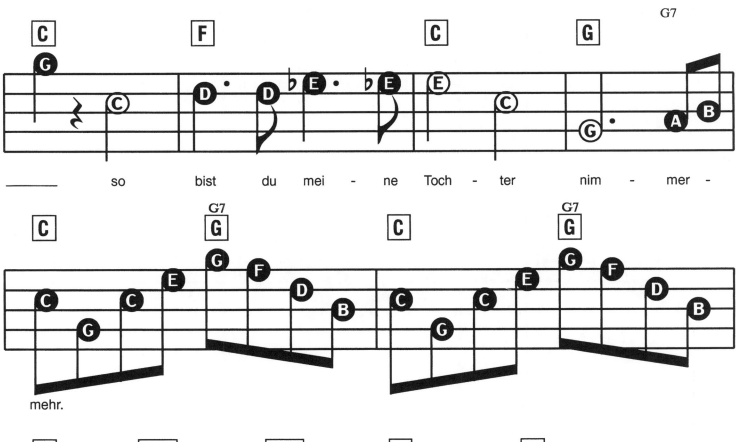

so bist du mei - ne Toch - ter nim - mer -

mehr.

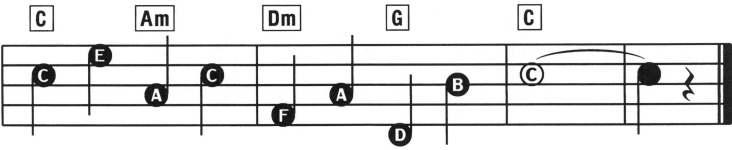

Habanera
from CARMEN

Registration 5
Rhythm: Latin or Tango

By Georges Bizet

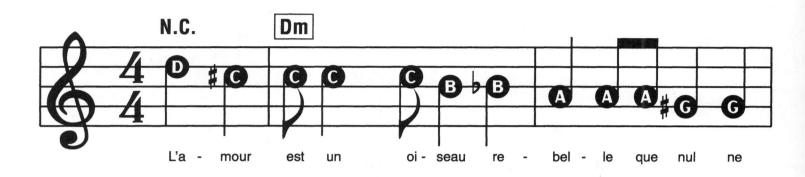

L'a - mour est un oi - seau re - bel - le que nul ne

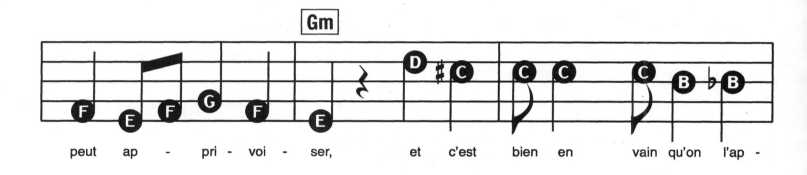

peut ap - pri - voi - ser, et c'est bien en vain qu'on l'ap -

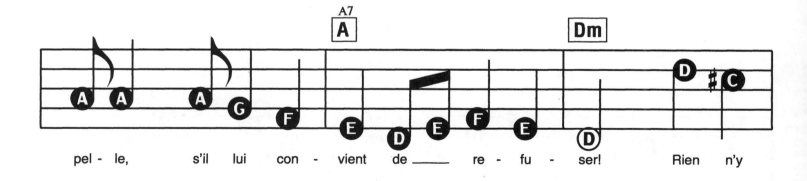

pel - le, s'il lui con - vient de ____ re - fu - ser! Rien n'y

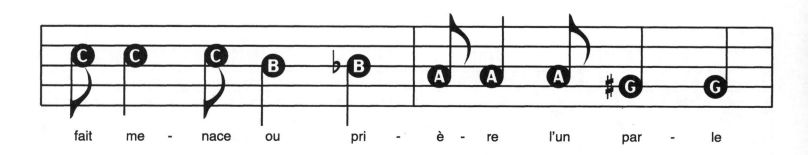

fait me - nace ou pri - è - re l'un par le

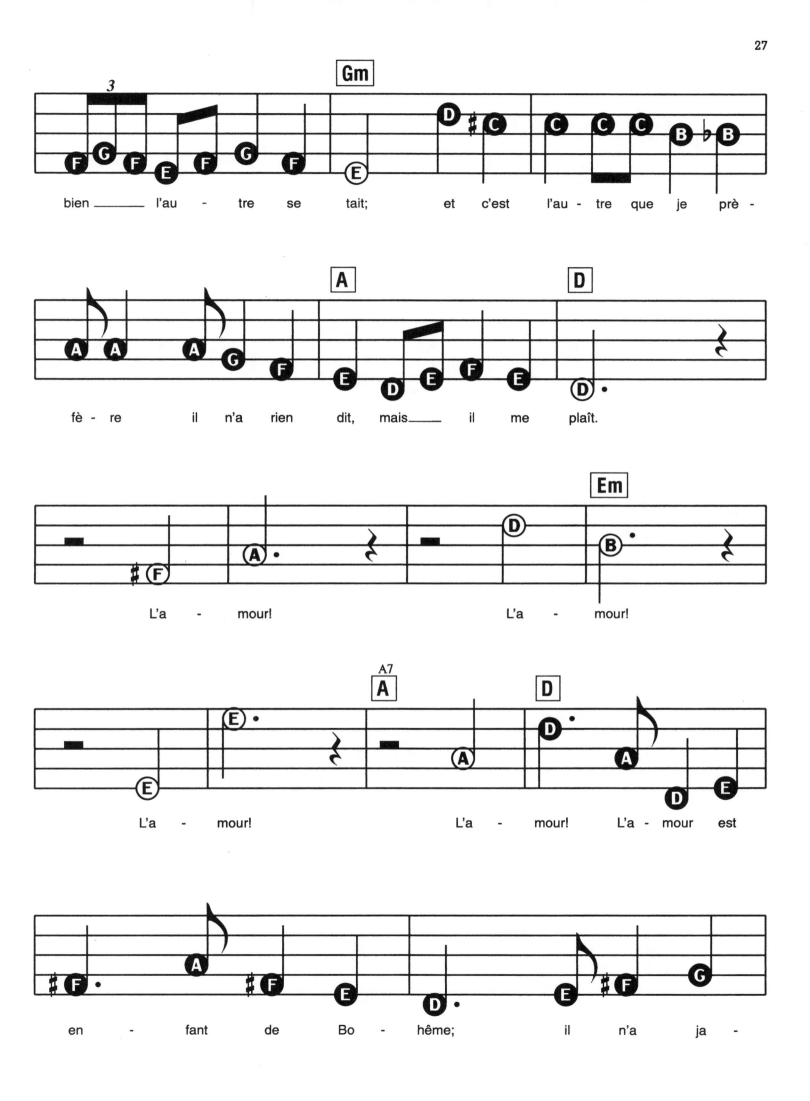

28

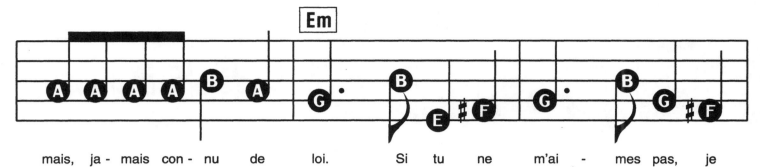

mais, ja - mais con - nu de loi.   Si   tu   ne   m'ai - mes pas,   je

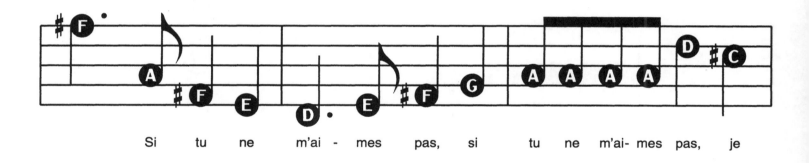

t'ai - me;   si   je t'ai - me, prends garde   à   toi!

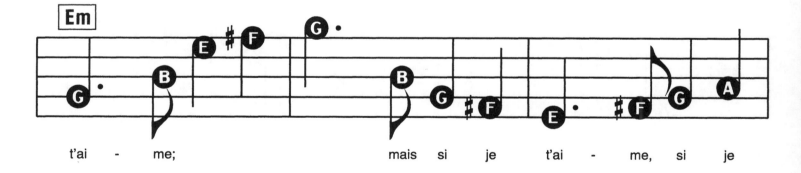

Si   tu   ne   m'ai - mes pas,   si   tu   ne m'ai - mes pas,   je

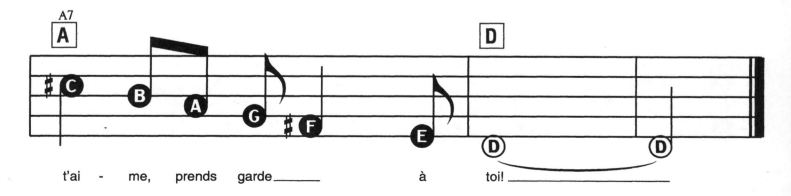

t'ai - me;   mais si   je   t'ai - me,   si   je

A7

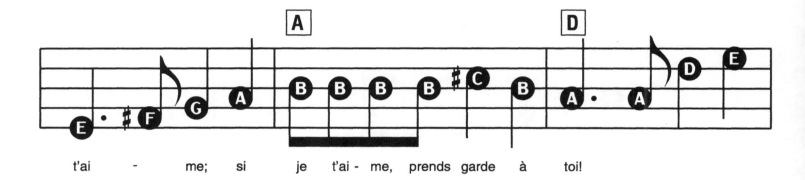

t'ai - me, prends garde_____   à   toi! _____

Là ci darem la mano
from DON GIOVANNI

Registration 1
Rhythm: 8-Beat

By Wolfgang Amadeus Mozart

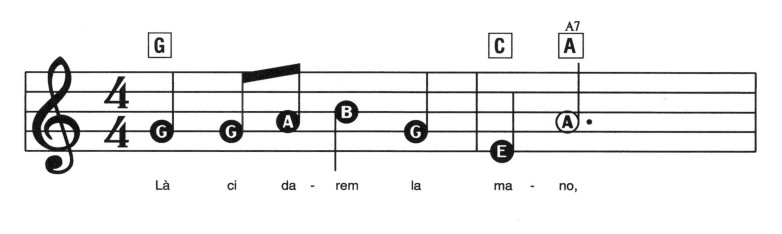

Là ci da - rem la ma - no,

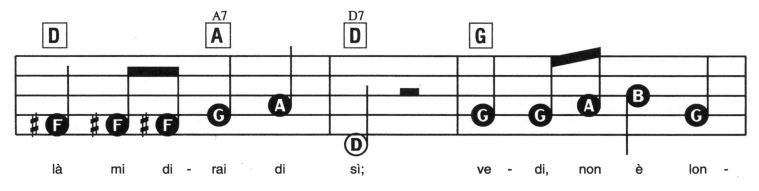

là mi di - rai di sì; ve - di, non è lon -

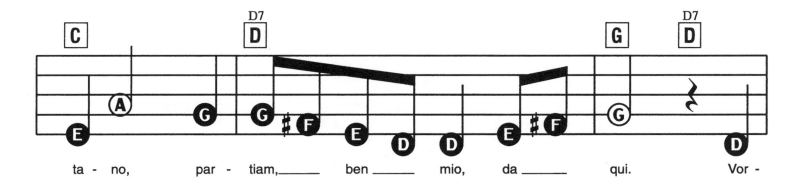

ta - no, par - tiam,____ ben ____ mio, da ____ qui. Vor -

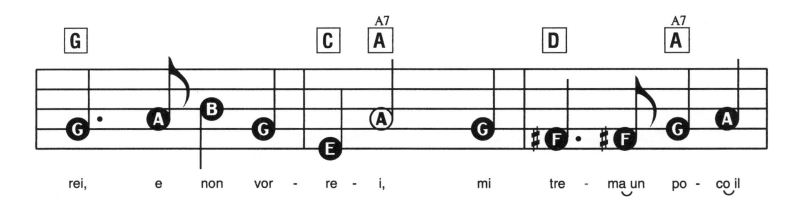

rei, e non vor - re - i, mi tre - ma un po - co il

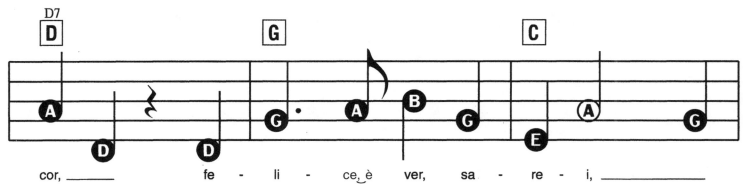

cor, _____ fe - li - ce, è ver, sa - re - i, _____

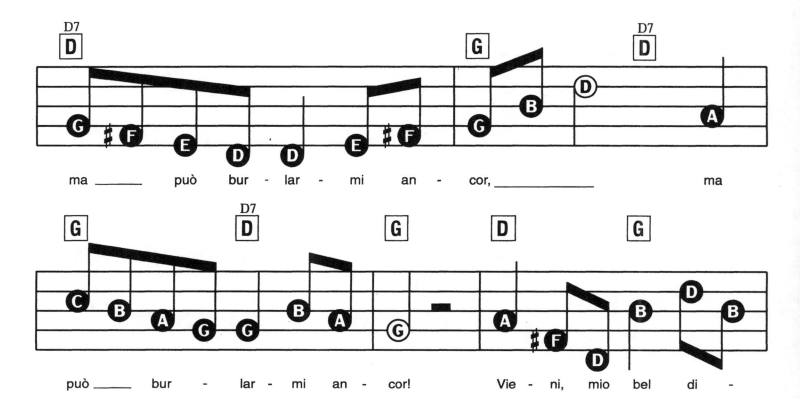

ma _____ può bur - lar - mi an - cor, _____ ma

può _____ bur - lar - mi an - cor! Vie - ni, mio bel di -

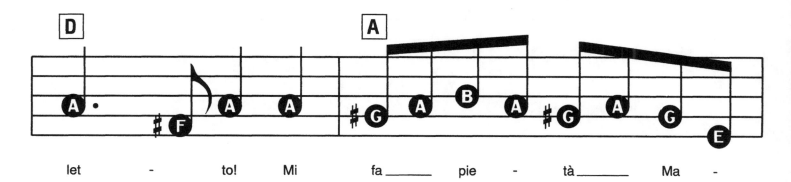

let - to! Mi fa_____ pie - tà_____ Ma -

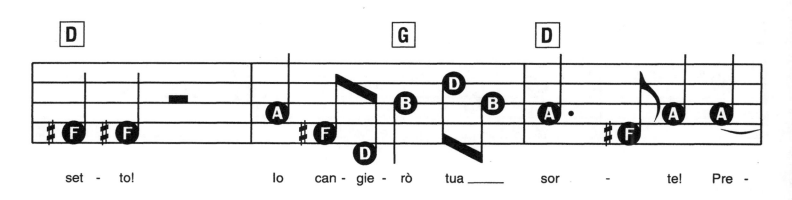

set - to! Io can - gie - rò tua _____ sor - te! Pre -

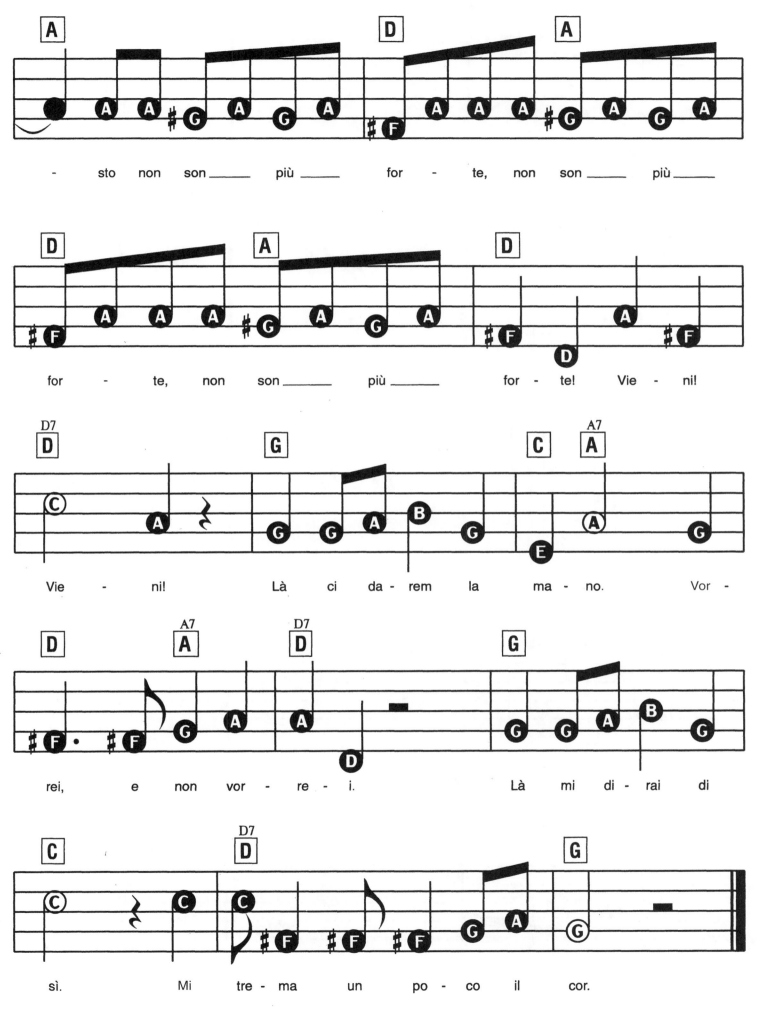

Intermezzo
from CAVALLERIA RUSTICANA

Registration 3
Rhythm: Waltz or None

By Pietro Mascagni

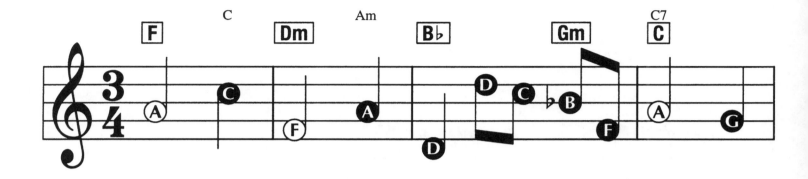

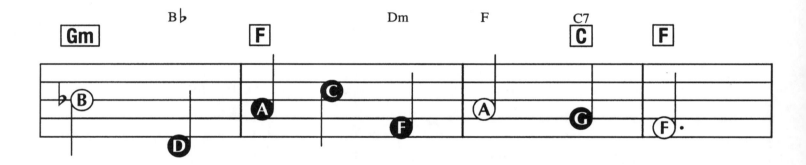

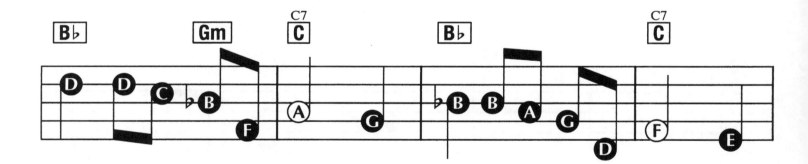

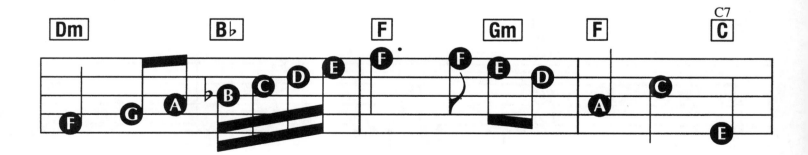

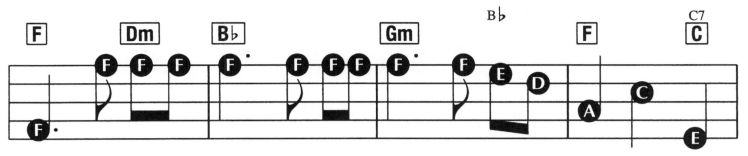

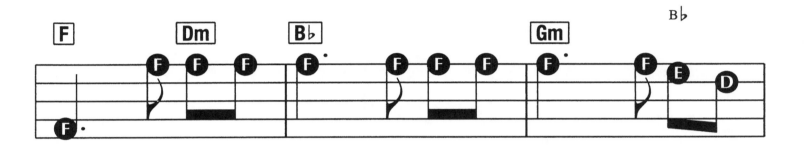

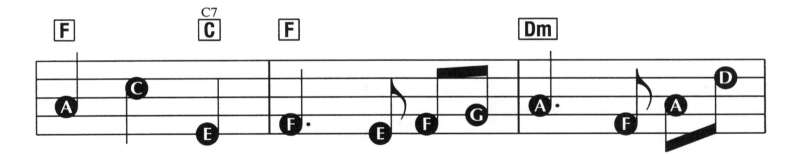

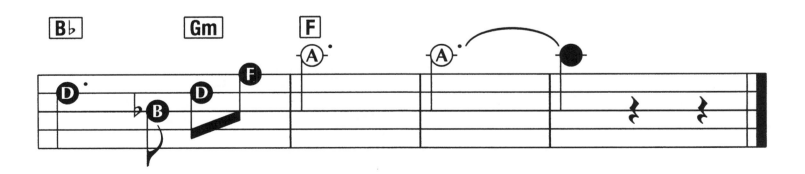

La donna è mobile

from RIGOLETTO

Registration 4
Rhythm: Waltz

By Giuseppe Verdi

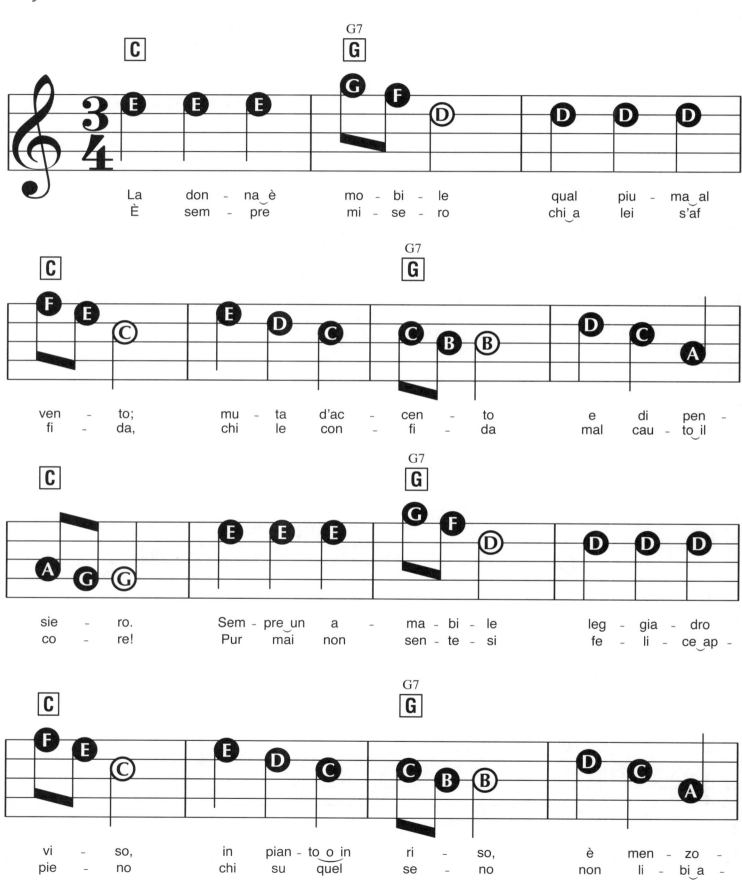

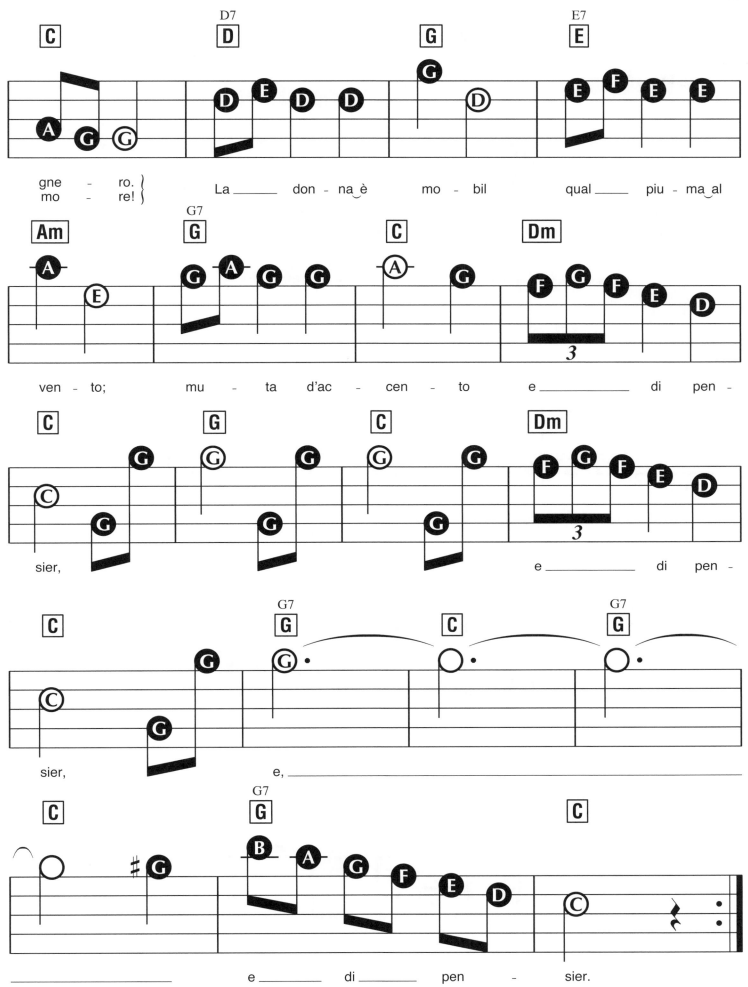

Libiamo
(The Drinking Song)
from LA TRAVIATA

Registration 7
Rhythm: Waltz

By Giuseppe Verdi

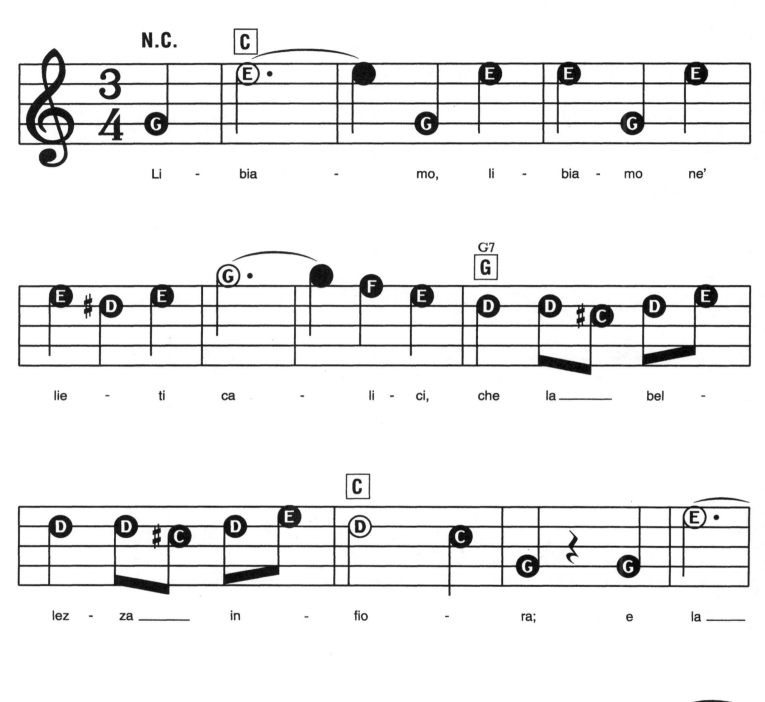

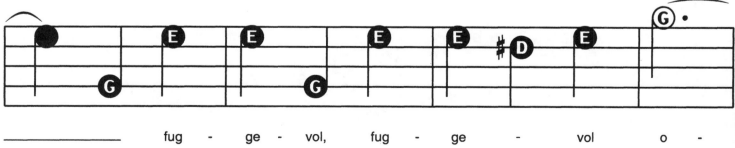

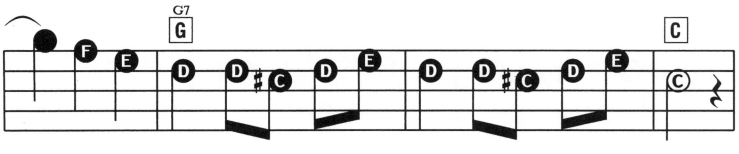

- ra s'i - ne - brii _____ a _____ vo - lu - tà.

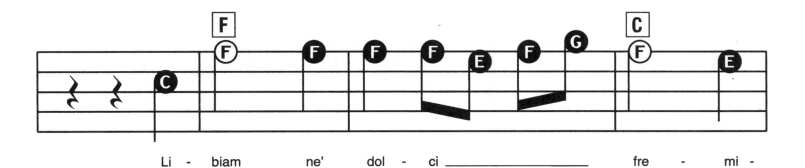

Li - biam ne' dol - ci _____ fre - mi -

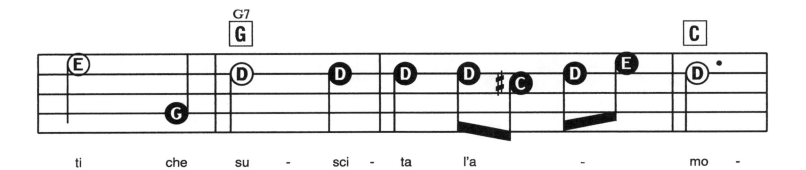

ti che su - sci - ta l'a - mo -

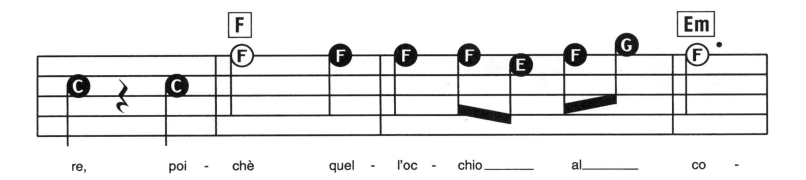

re, poi - chè quel - l'oc - chio _____ al _____ co -

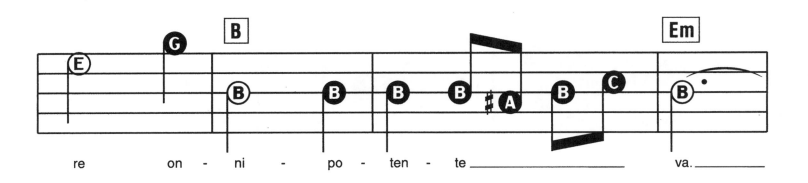

re on - ni - po - ten - te _____ va. _____

38

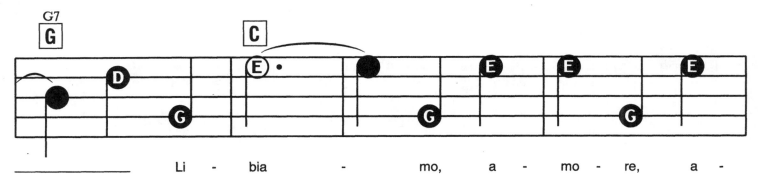

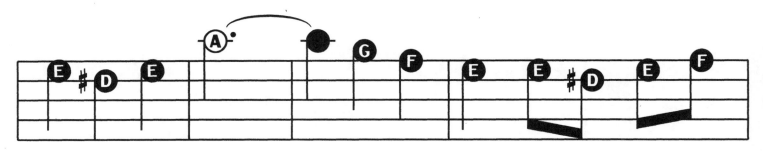

Li - bia - mo, a - mo - re, a -

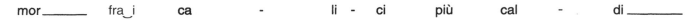

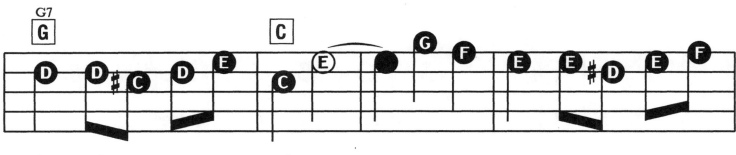

mor_____ fra_i ca - li - ci più cal - di_____

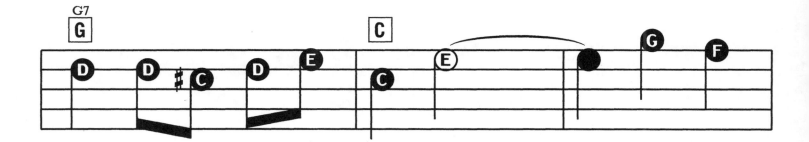

ba - ci_____ a - vrà.

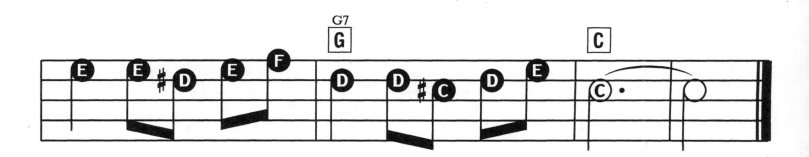

Non più andrai
from LE NOZZE DI FIGARO

Registration 4
Rhythm: Swing or Shuffle

By Wolfgang Amadeus Mozart

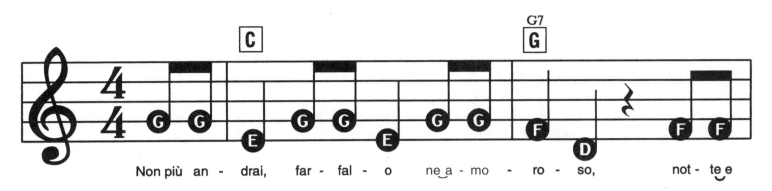

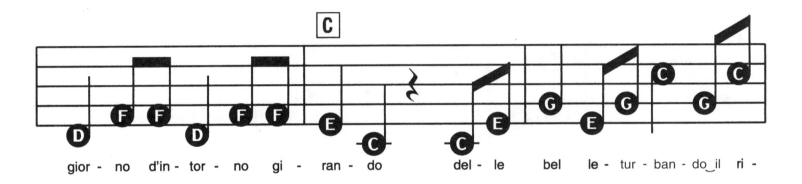

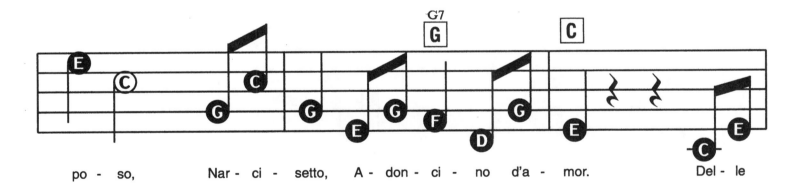

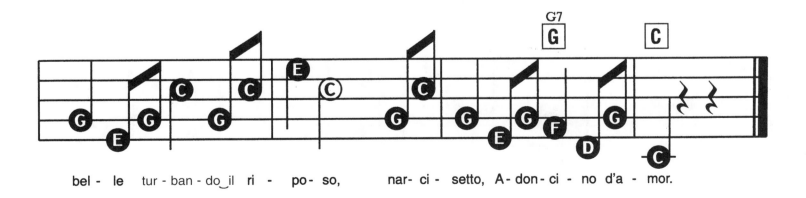

M'appari tutt' amor
from MARTHA

Registration 10
Rhythm: None

By Friedrich Flotow

41

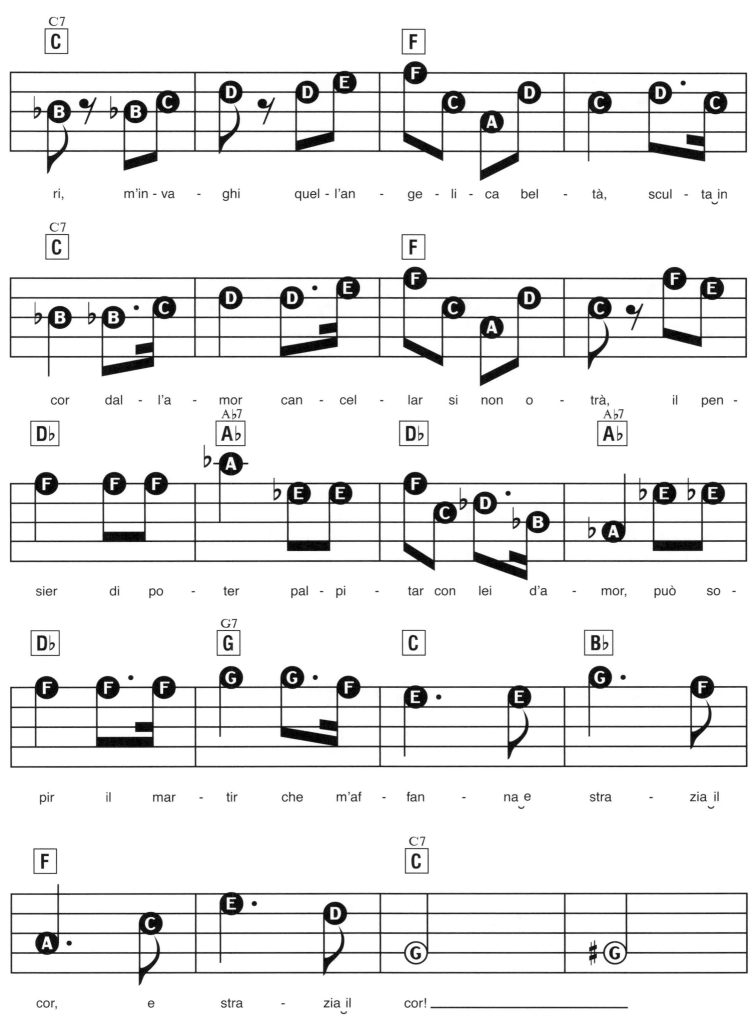

42

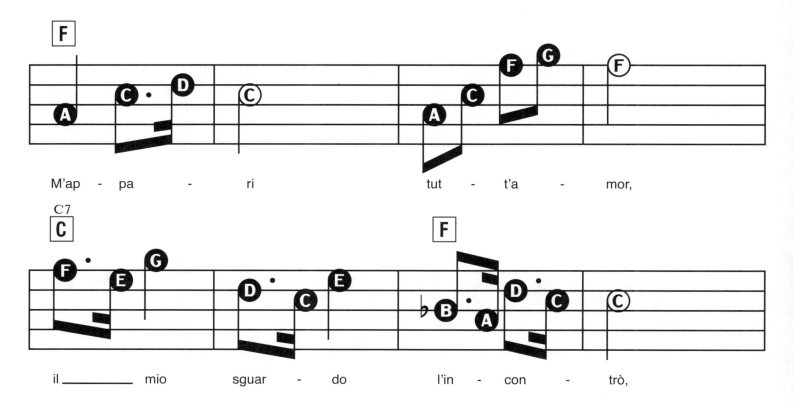

M'ap - pa - ri   tut - t'a - mor,

il _____ mio sguar - do l'in - con - trò,

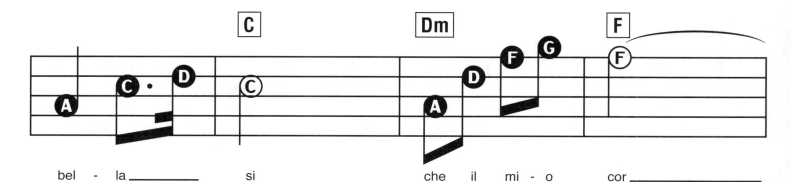

bel - la _____ si   che il mi - o cor _____

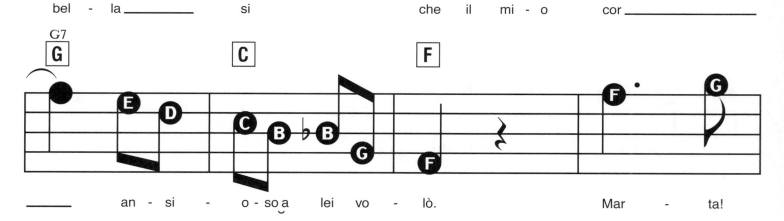

_____ an - si - o - so a lei vo - lò.   Mar - ta!

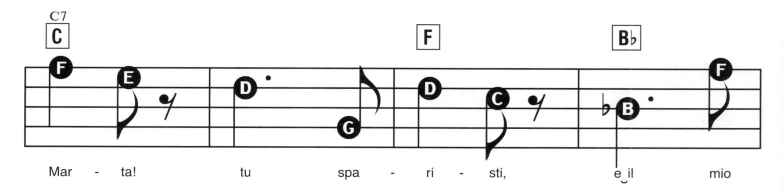

Mar - ta!   tu spa - ri - sti,   e il mio

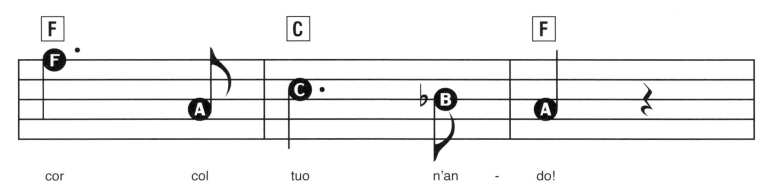

cor   col   tuo   n'an - do!

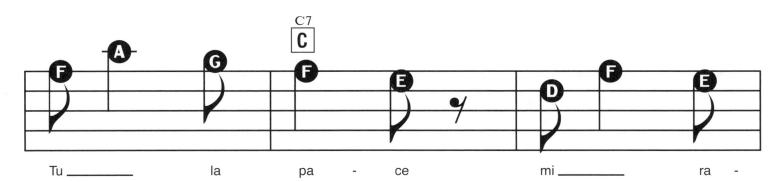

Tu   la   pa - ce   mi   ra -

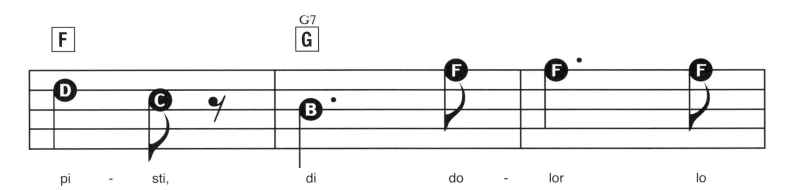

pi - sti,   di   do - lor   lo

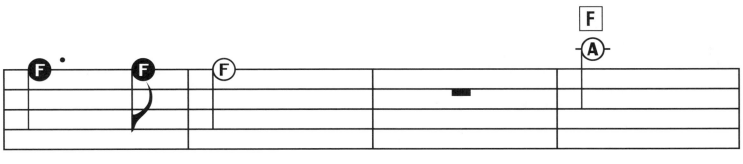

mo - ri - rò,   ah!

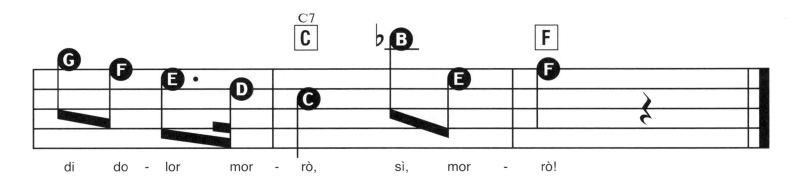

di do - lor mor - rò,   sì, mor - rò!

Meditation
from THAÏS

Registration 3
Rhythm: Ballad

By Jules Massenet

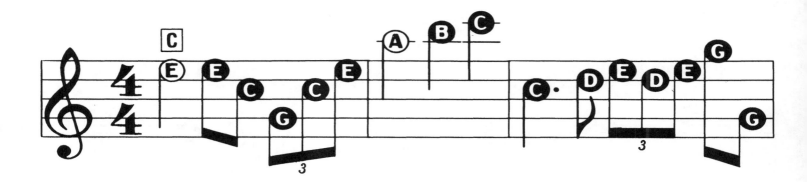

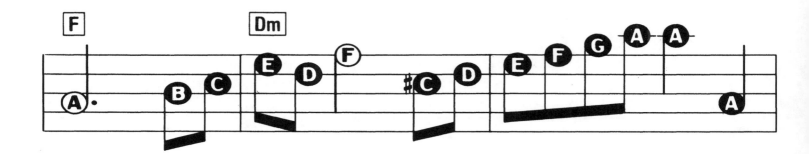

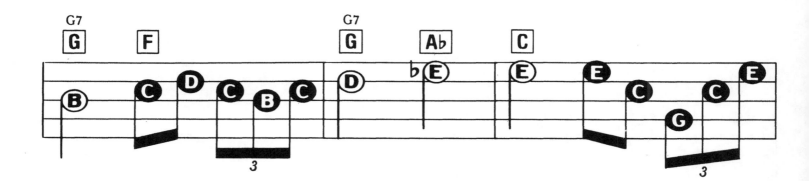

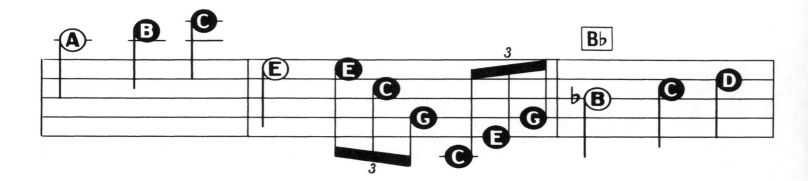

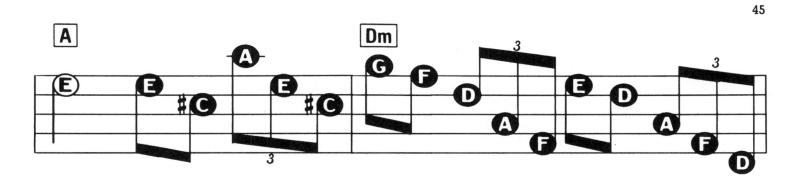

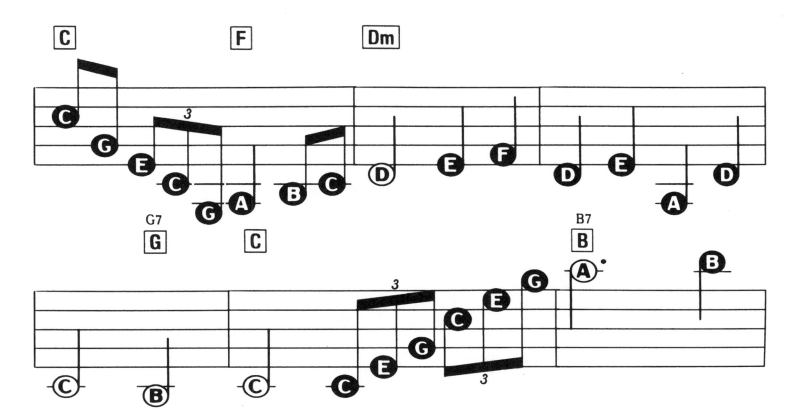

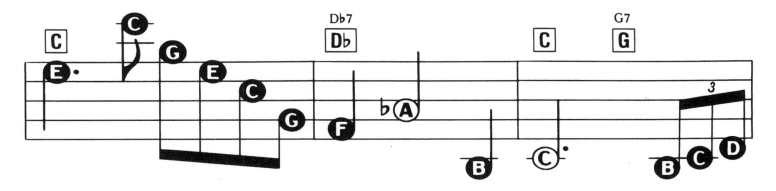

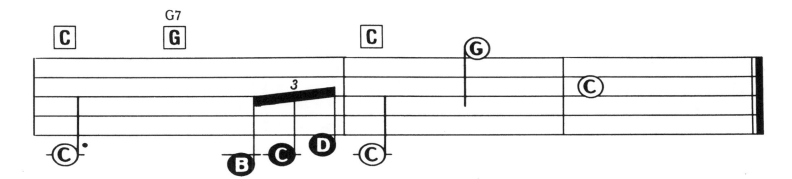

Minuet
from DON GIOVANNI

Registration 3
Rhythm: Waltz

By Wolfgang Amadeus Mozart

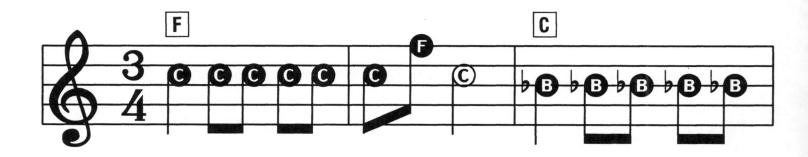

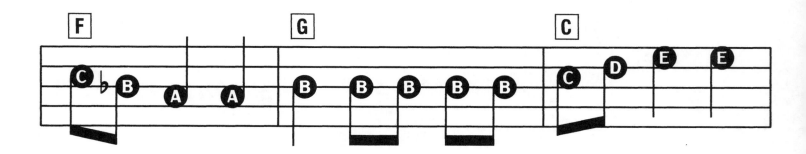

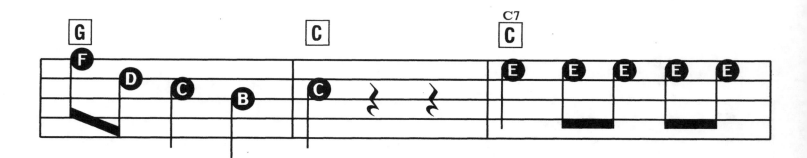

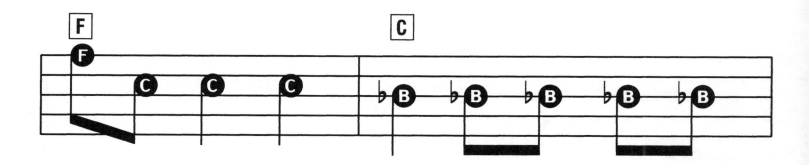

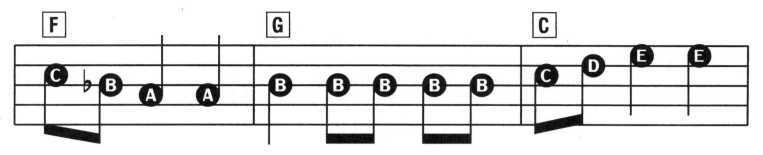

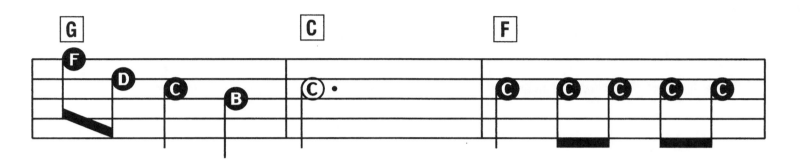

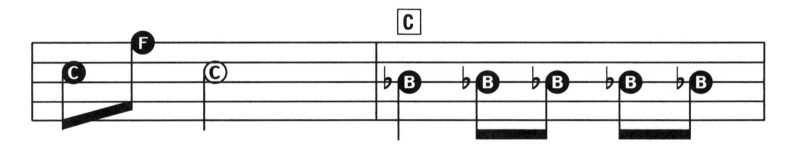

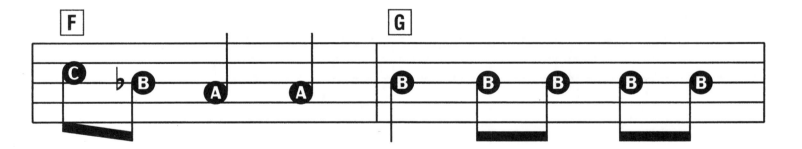

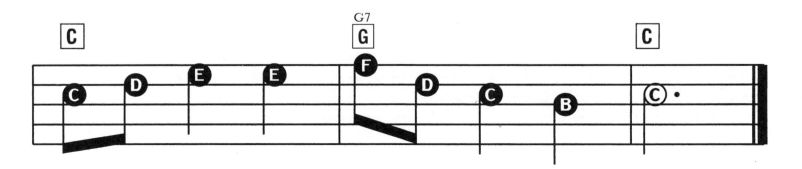

O mio babbino caro

from GIANNI SCHICCHI

Registration 3
Rhythm: Waltz

By Giacomo Puccini

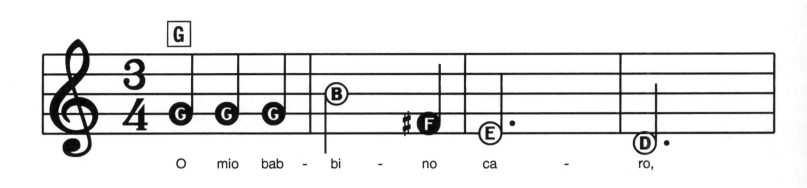

O mio bab - bi - no ca - ro,

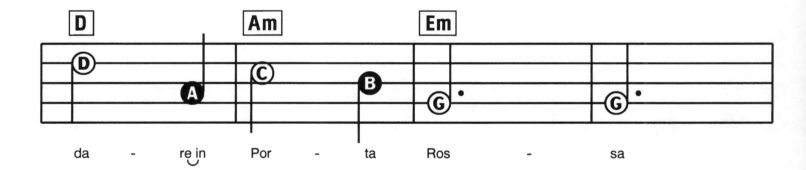

mi pia - ce,è bel - lo, bel - lo; vo' an -

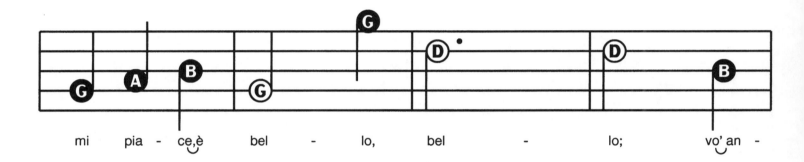

da - re in Por - ta Ros - sa

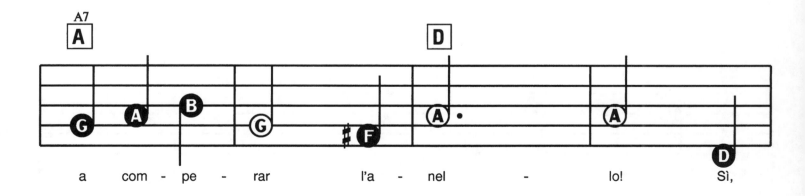

a com - pe - rar l'a - nel - lo! Sì,

49

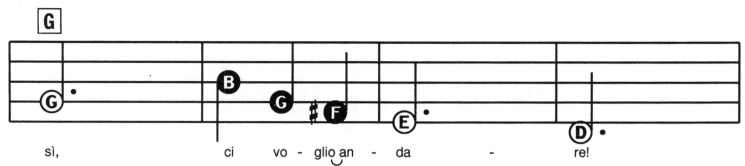

sì,   ci vo - glio an - da   -   re!

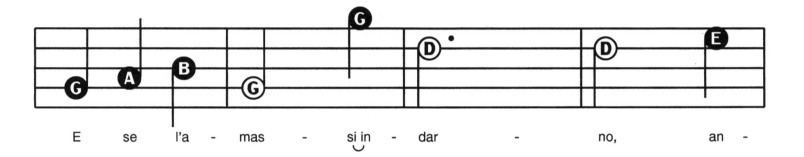

E se l'a - mas - si in dar   -   no,   an -

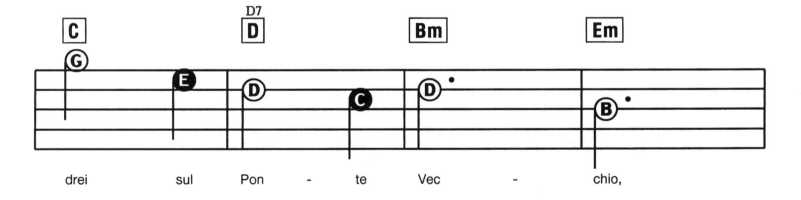

drei   sul   Pon - te Vec -   chio,

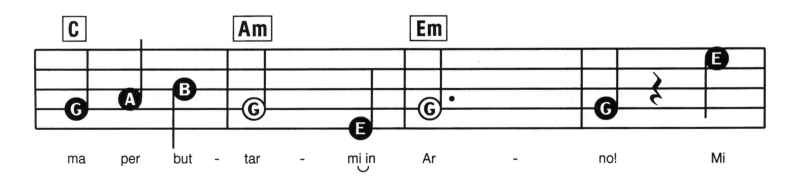

ma per but - tar - mi in Ar   -   no!   Mi

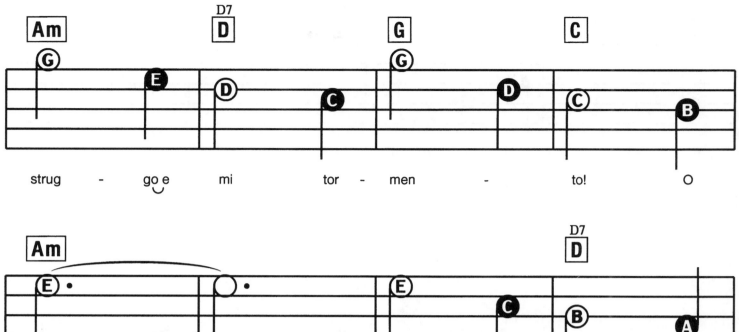

strug - go e mi tor - men - to! O

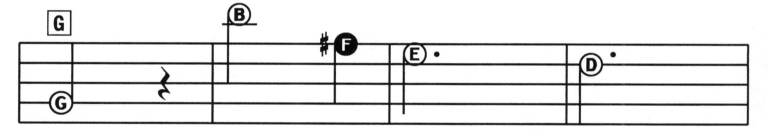

Di - o, vor - rei mo -

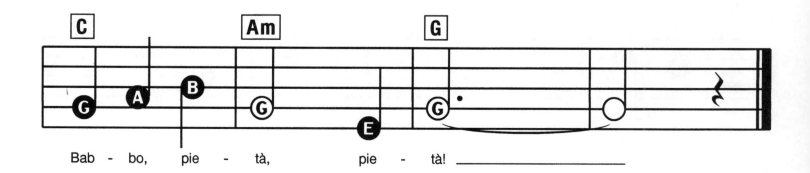

rir!

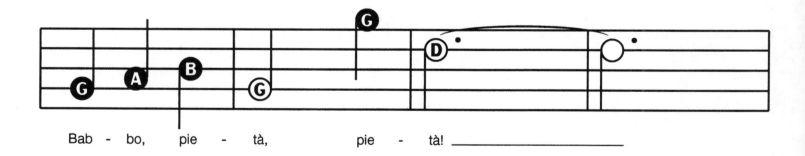

Bab - bo, pie - tà, pie - tà! _____

Bab - bo, pie - tà, pie - tà! _____

O soave fanciulla
from LA BOHÈME

Registration 3
Rhythm: Ballad

By Giacomo Puccini

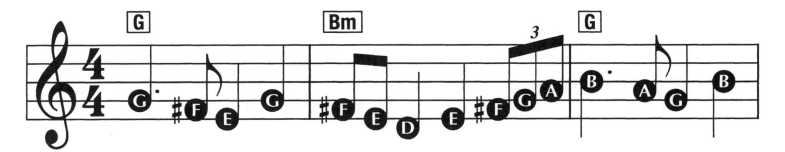

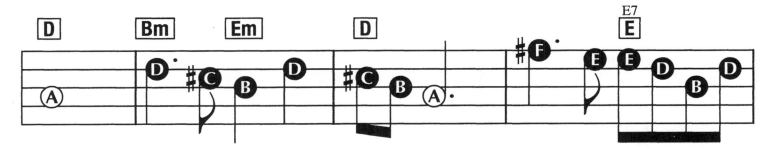

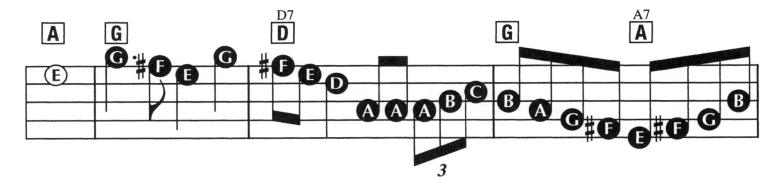

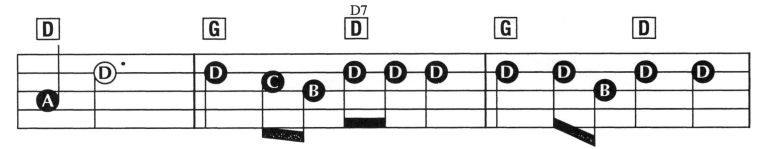

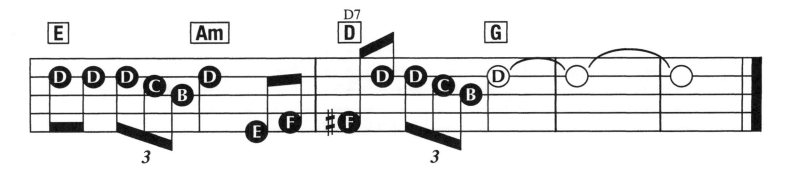

Pilgrims' Chorus
from TANNHÄUSER

Registration 6
Rhythm: Waltz

By Richard Wagner

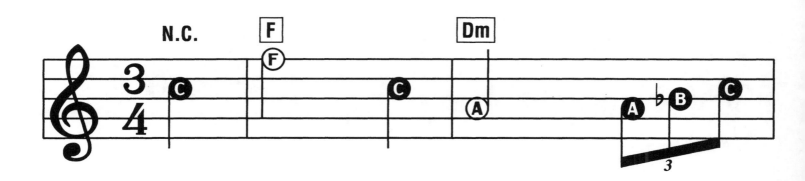

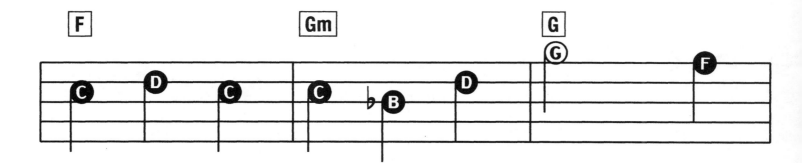

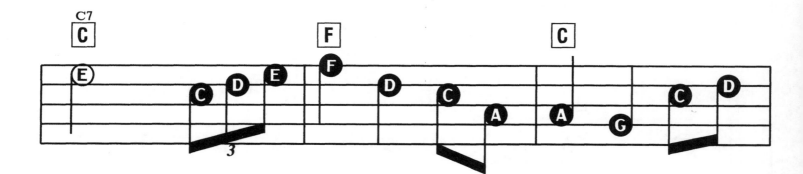

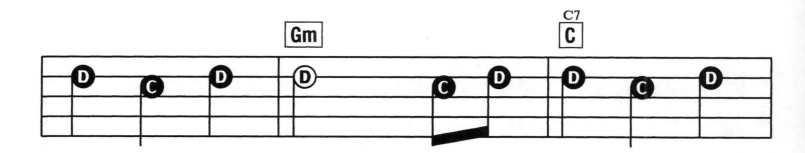

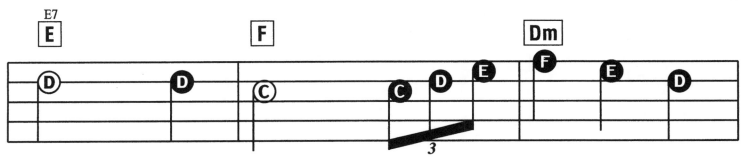

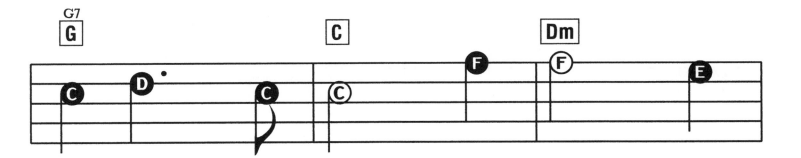

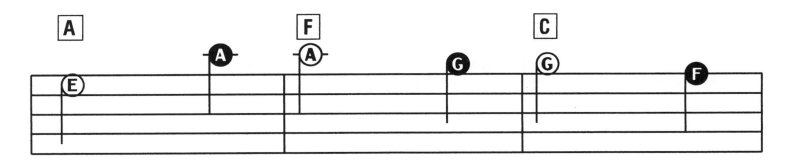

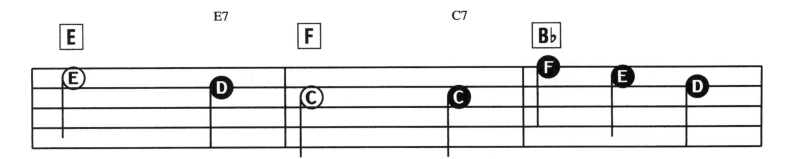

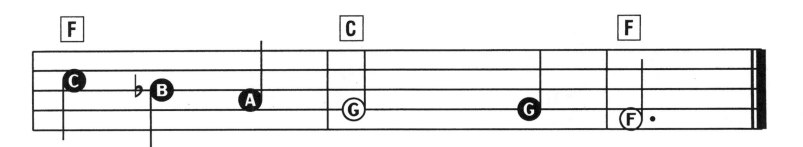

Quando men vo
(Musetta's Waltz)
from LA BOHÈME

Registration 3
Rhythm: Waltz

By Giacomo Puccini

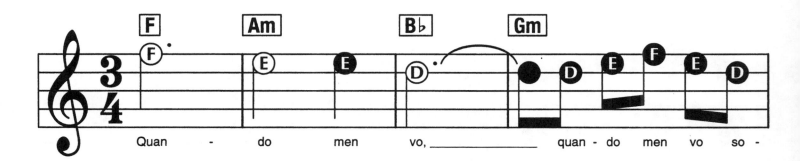

Quan - do men vo, _____ quan - do men vo so -

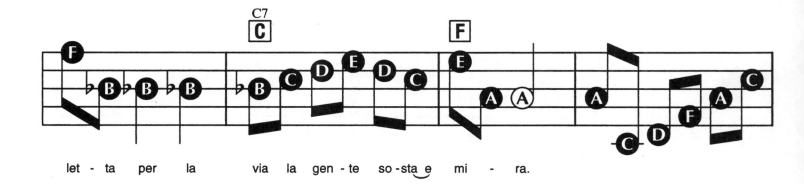

let - ta per la via la gen - te so - sta e mi - ra.

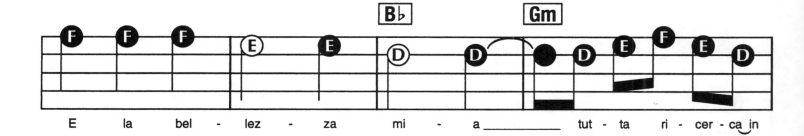

E la bel - lez - za mi - a _____ tut - ta ri - cer - ca in

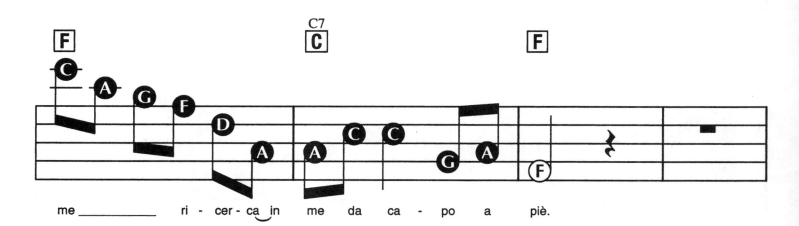

me _____ ri - cer - ca in me da ca - po a piè.

55

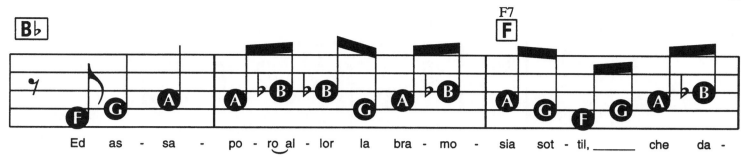

Ed as - sa - po - ro al - lor la bra - mo - sia sot - til, _____ che da -

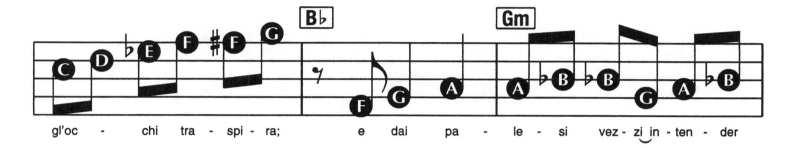

gl'oc - chi tra - spi - ra; e dai pa - le - si vez - zi in - ten - der

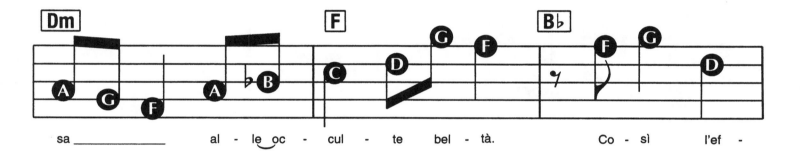

sa _____ al - le oc - cul - te bel - tà. Co - sì l'ef -

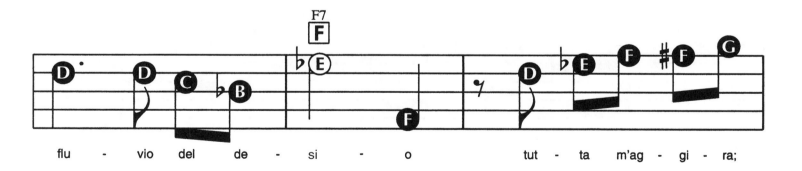

flu - vio del de - si - o tut - ta m'ag - gi - ra;

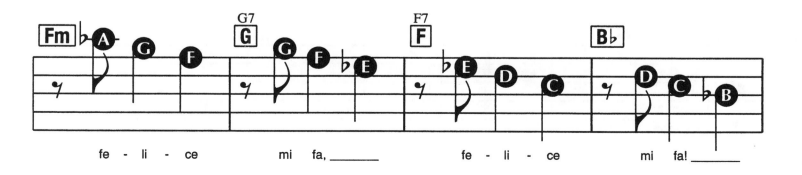

fe - li - ce mi fa, _____ fe - li - ce mi fa! _____

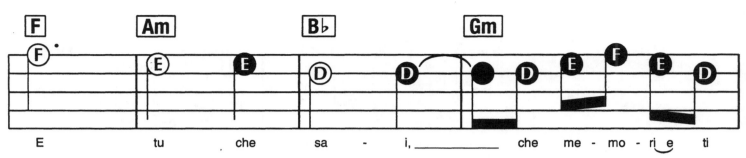

E   tu   che   sa   -   i, _____ che me - mo - ri_e ti

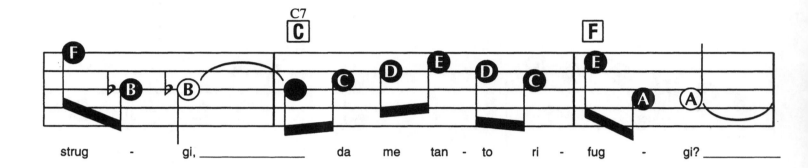

strug   -   gi, _____ da me tan - to ri - fug - gi? _____

_____   So   ben: le_an - go - scie   tue   non   le   vuoi

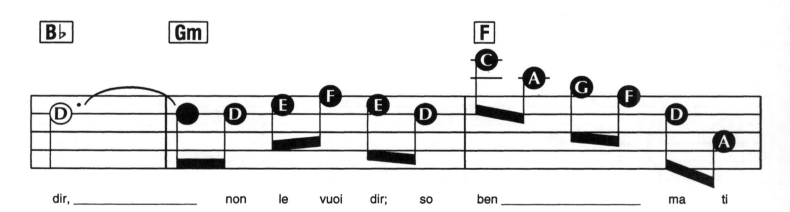

dir, _____ non le vuoi dir; so ben _____ ma ti

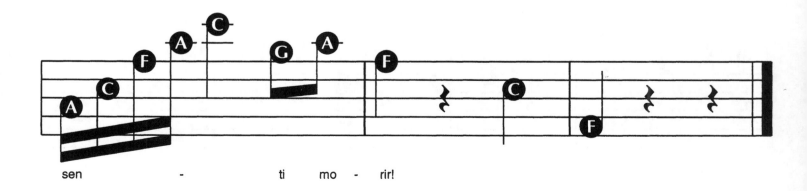

sen   -   ti mo - rir!

Questa o quella
from RIGOLETTO

Registration 4
Rhythm: 6/8 March

By Giuseppe Verdi

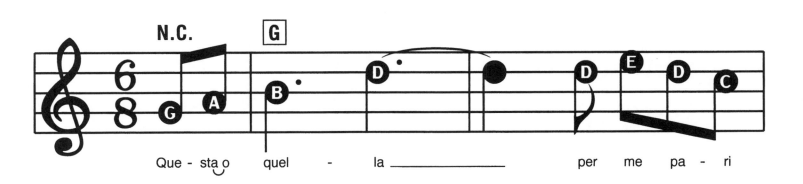

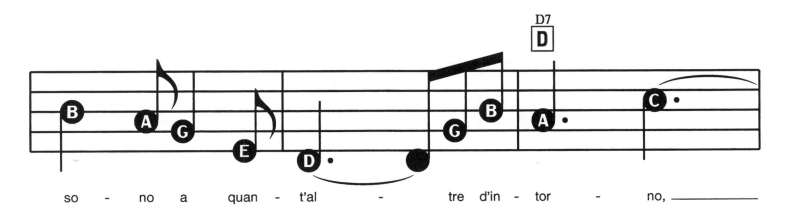

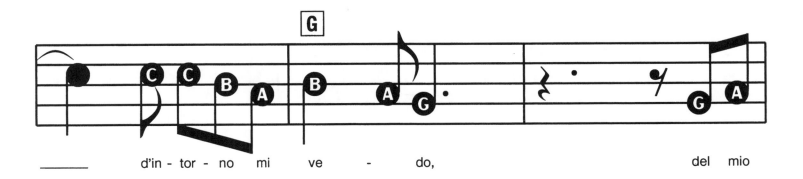

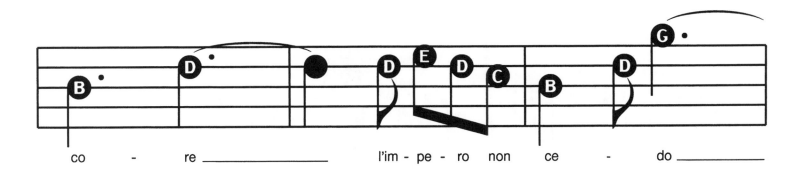

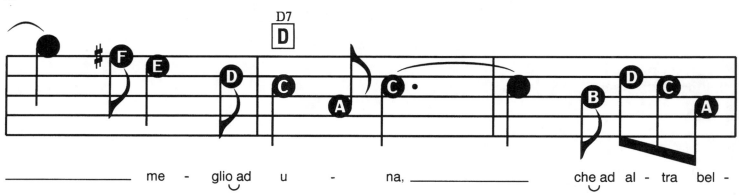

me - glio ad u - na, _____ che ad al - tra bel -

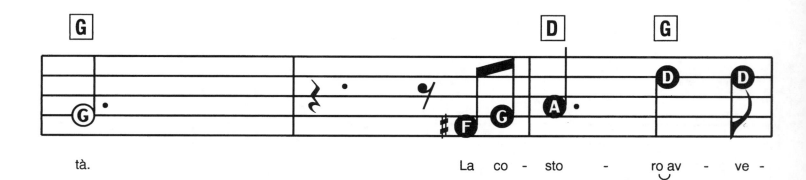

tà. La co - sto - ro av - ve -

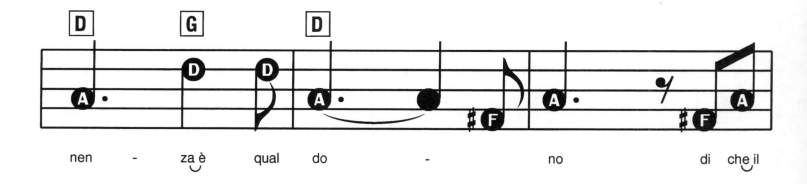

nen - za è qual do - no di che il

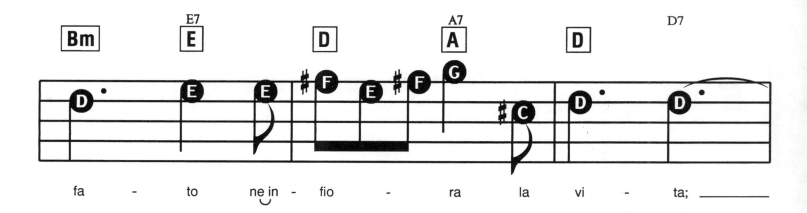

fa - to ne in - fio - ra la vi - ta; _____

59

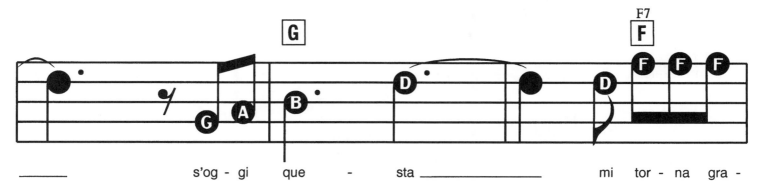

s'og - gi que - sta _____ mi tor - na gra -

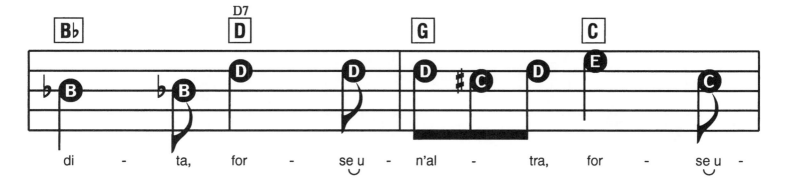

di - ta, for - se u - n'al - tra, for - se u -

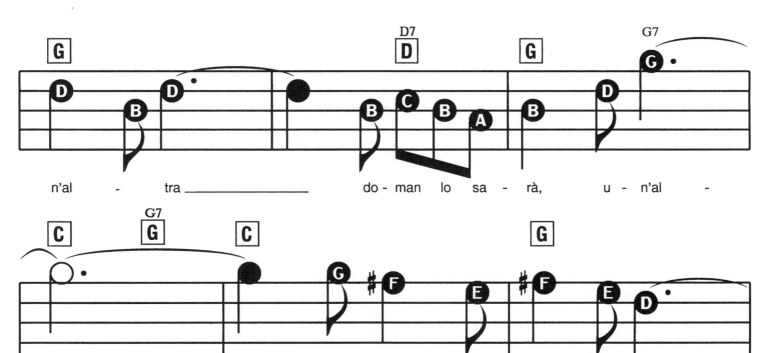

n'al - tra _____ do - man lo sa - rà, u - n'al -

tra, for - se u - n'al - tra _____

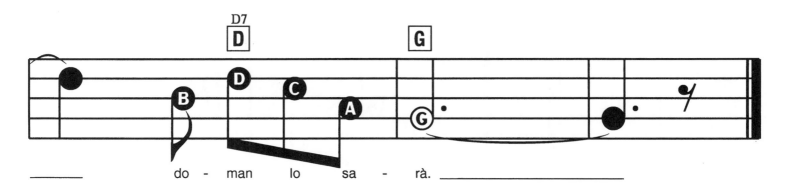

do - man lo sa - rà. _____

Ride of the Valkyries
from DIE WALKÜRE

Registration 2
Rhythm: Waltz

By Richard Wagner

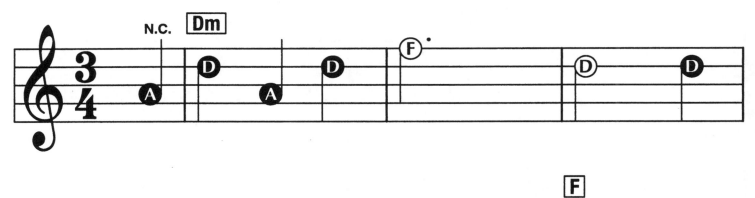

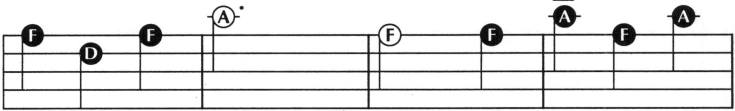

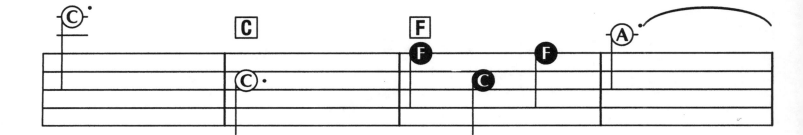

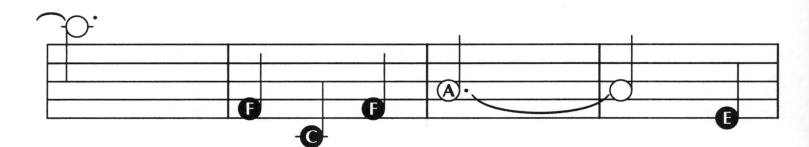

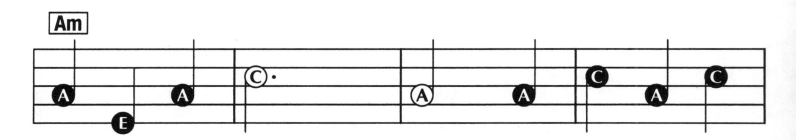

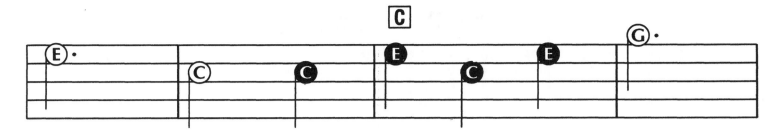

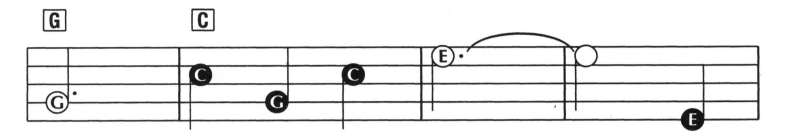

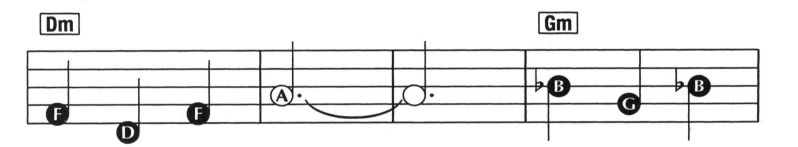

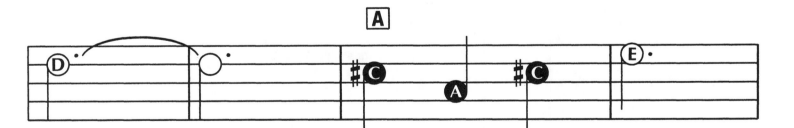

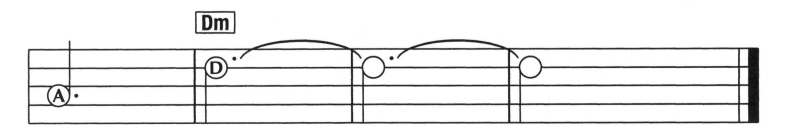

Seguidilla
from CARMEN

Registration 4
Rhythm: Waltz

By Georges Bizet

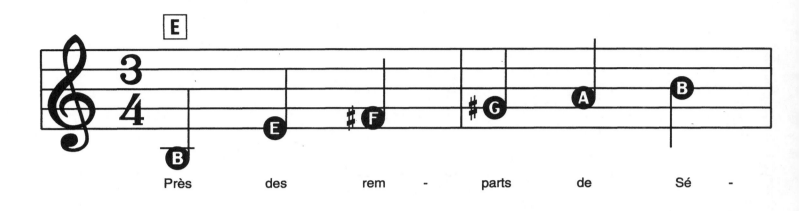

Près des rem - parts de Sé -

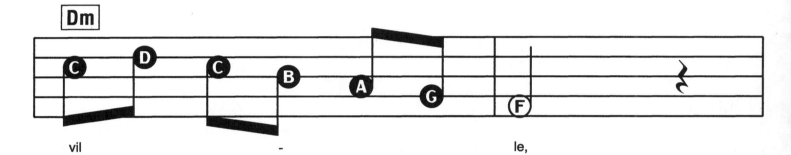

vil - le,

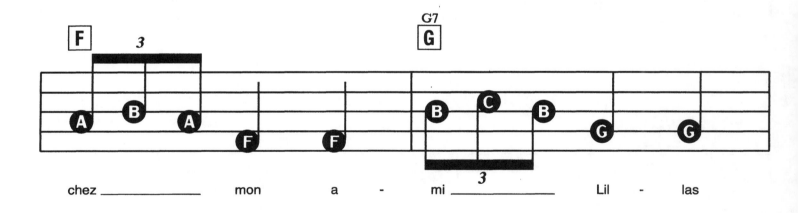

chez _____ mon a - mi _____ Lil - las

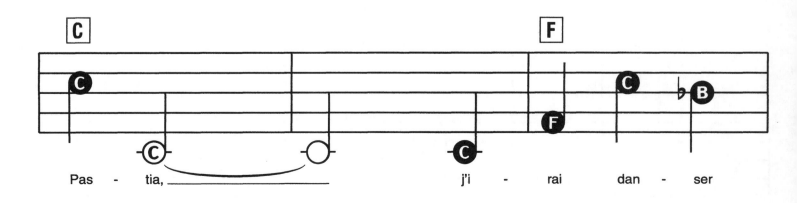

Pas - tia, _____ j'i - rai dan - ser

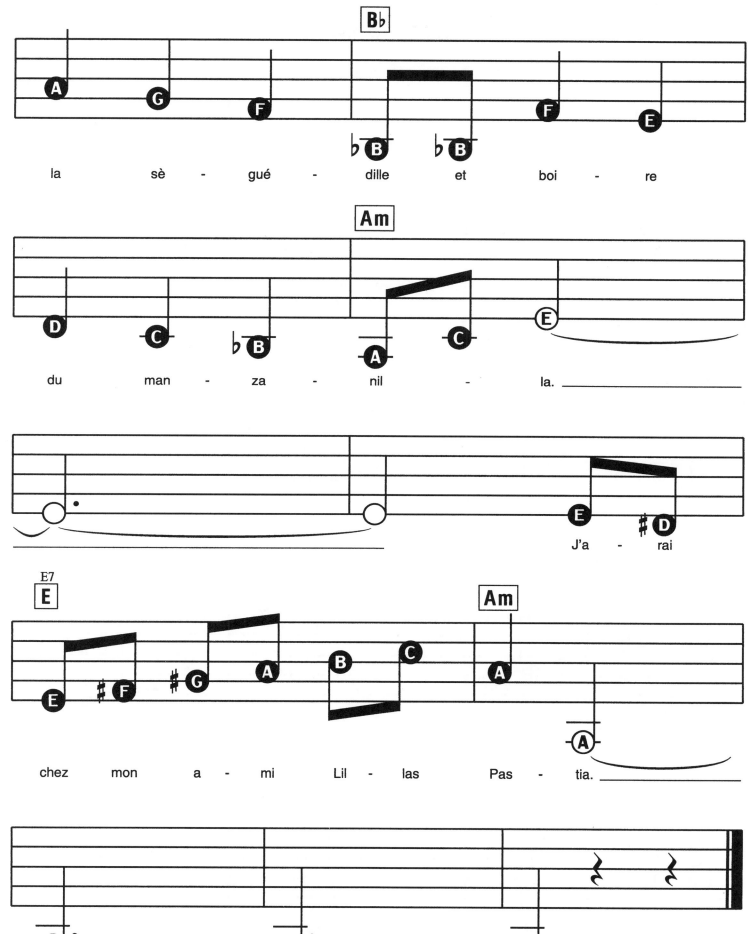

Sola, perduta, abbandonata
from MANON LESCAUT

Registration 3
Rhythm: Ballad

By Giacomo Puccini

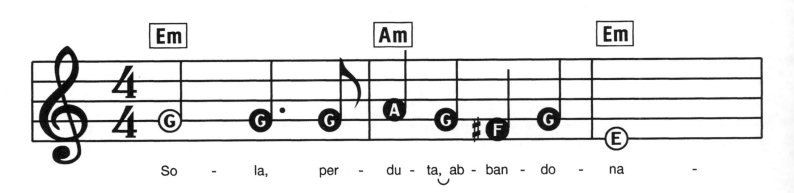

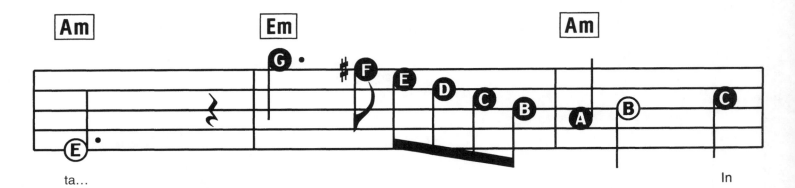

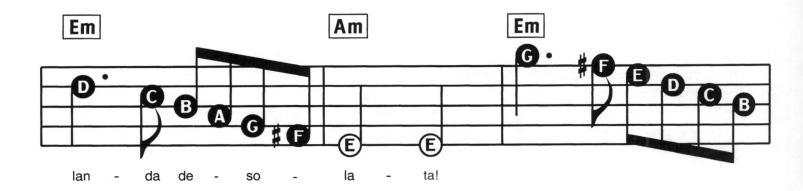

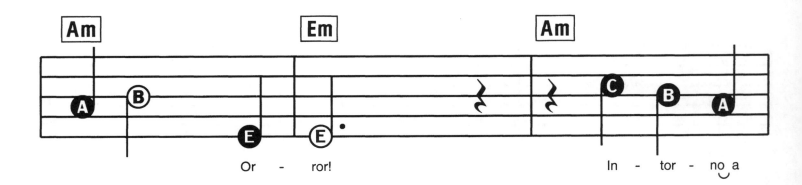

65

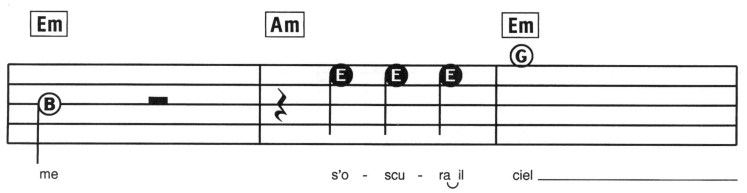

me   s'o - scu - ra il   ciel _____

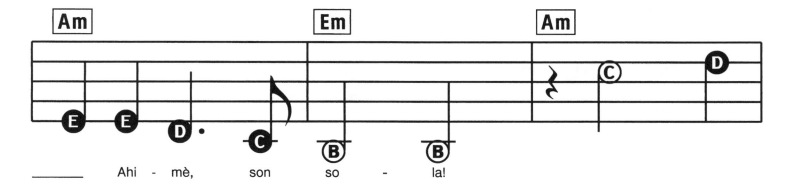

_____   Ahi - mè,   son   so -   la!

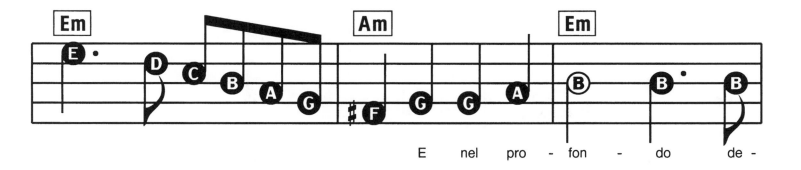

E   nel   pro - fon - do   de -

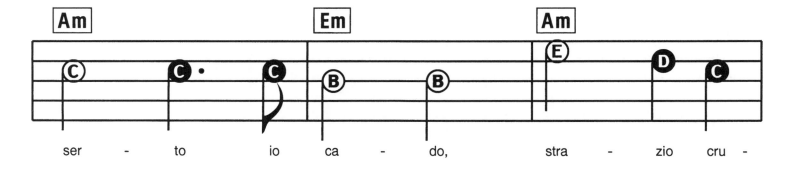

ser -   to   io   ca -   do,   stra -   zio   cru -

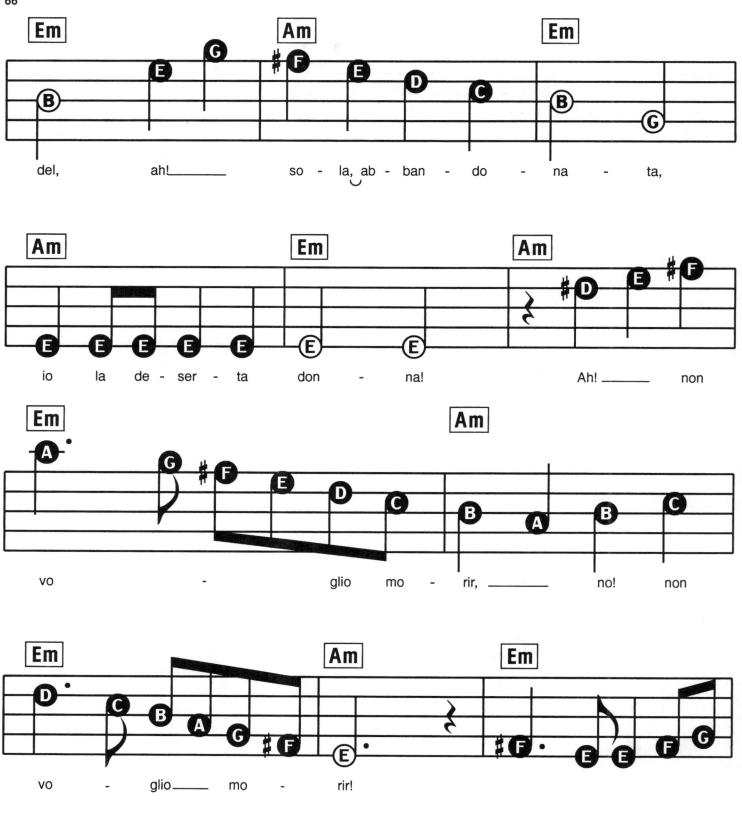

del, ah! _____ so - la, ab - ban - do - na - ta,

io la de - ser - ta don - na! Ah! _____ non

vo - glio mo - rir, _____ no! non

vo - glio _____ mo - rir!

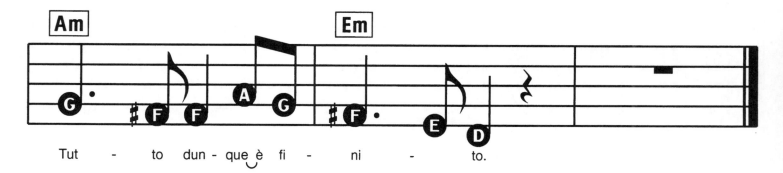

Tut - to dun - que è fi - ni - to.

Una furtiva lagrima
from L'ELISIR D'AMORE

Registration 1
Rhythm: Waltz or None

By Gaetano Donizetti

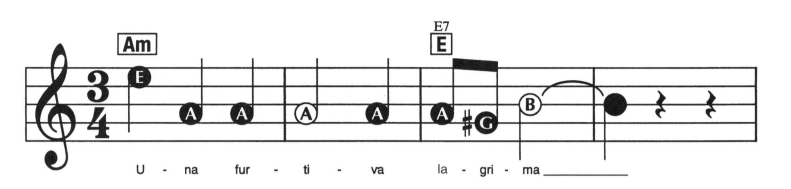

U - na fur - ti - va la - gri - ma _____

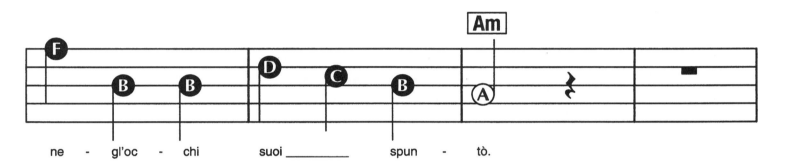

ne - gl'oc - chi suoi _____ spun - tò.

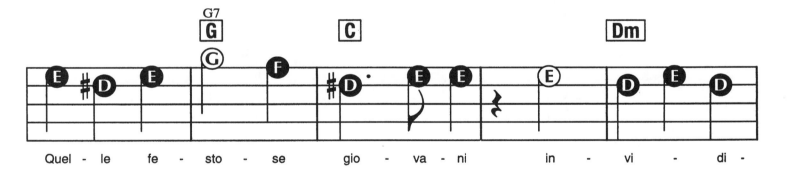

Quel - le fe - sto - se gio - va - ni in - vi - di -

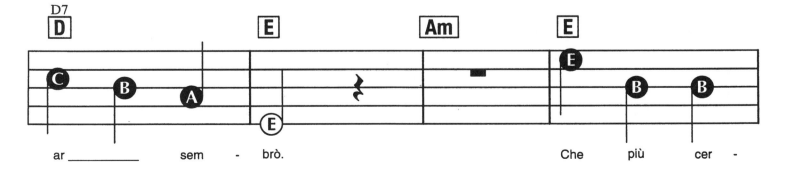

ar _____ sem - brò. Che più cer -

68

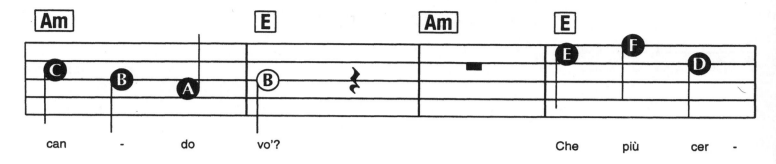

can - do vo'? Che più cer -

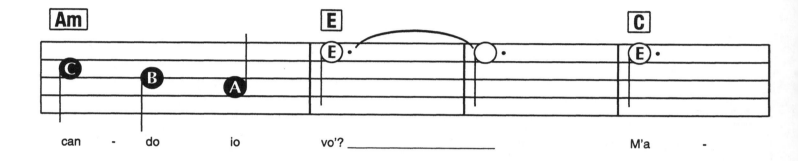

can - do io vo'? _____ M'a -

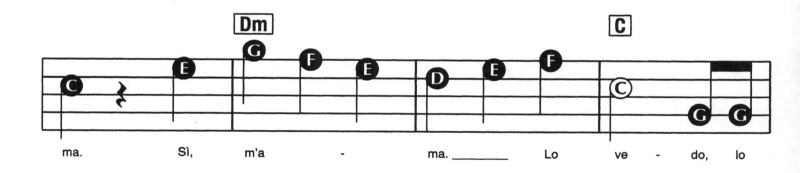

ma. Sì, m'a - ma. _____ Lo ve - do, lo

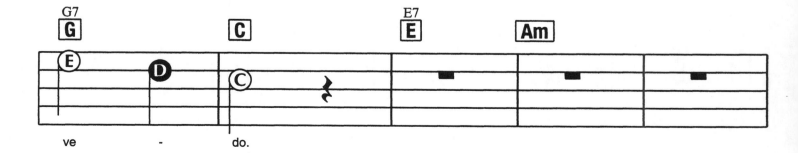

ve - do.

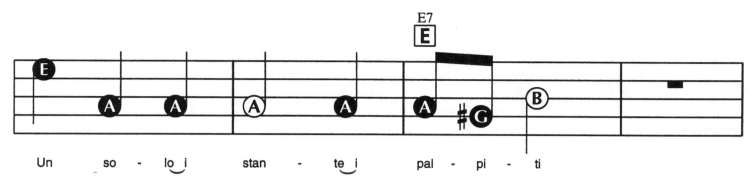

Un so - lo i stan - te i pal - pi - ti

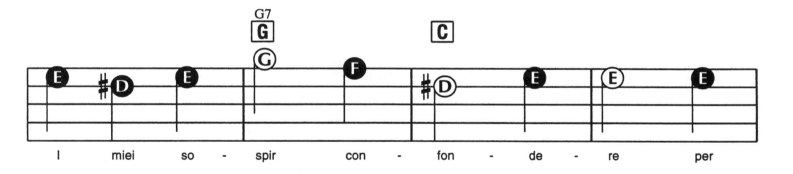

del suo bel cor _____ sen - tir!

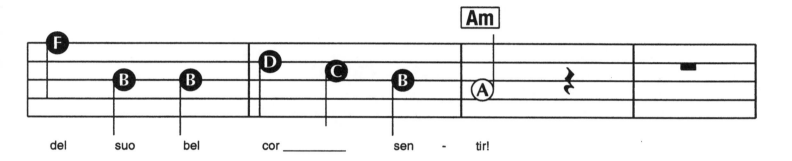

I miei so - spir con - fon - de - re per

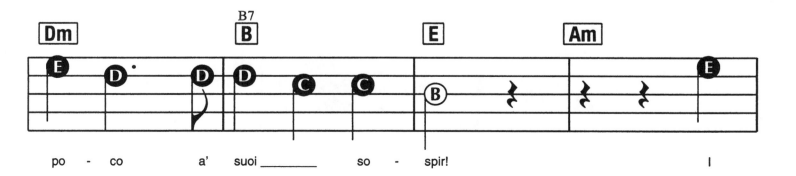

po - co a' suoi _____ so - spir! I

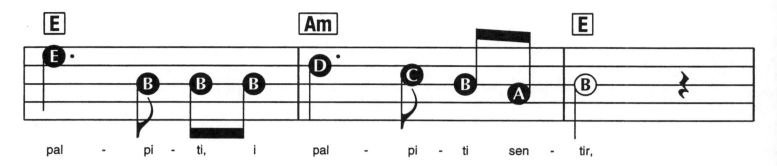

pal - pi - ti, i pal - pi - ti sen - tir,

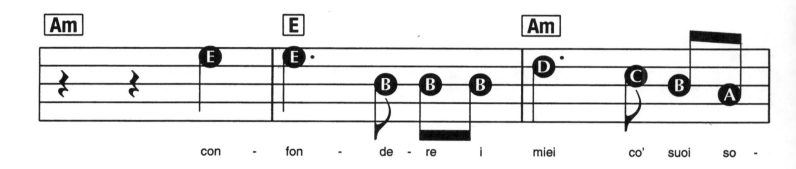

con - fon - de - re i miei co' suoi so -

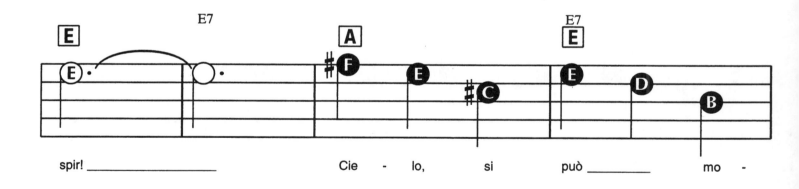

spir! _____ Cie - lo, si può _____ mo -

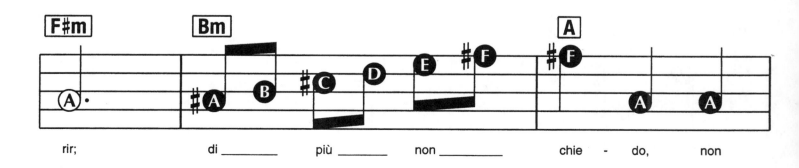

rir; di _____ più _____ non _____ chie - do, non

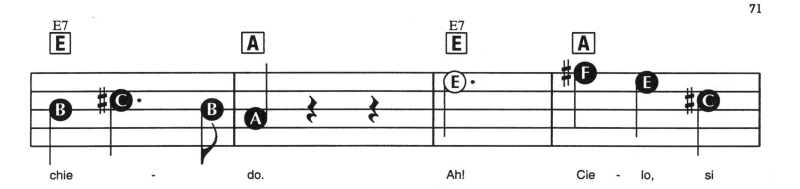

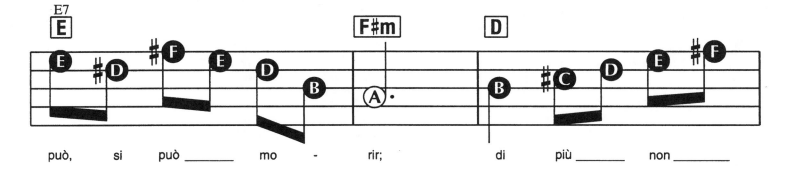

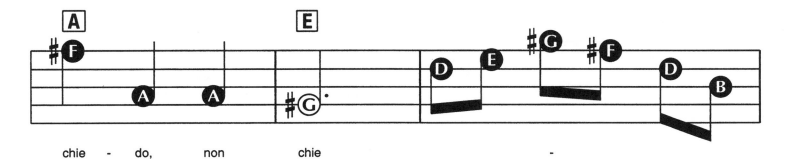

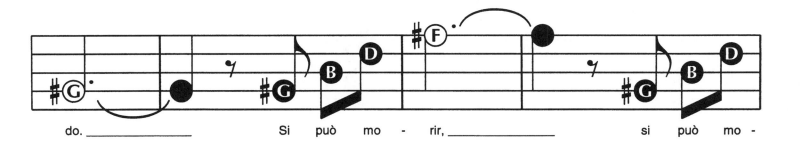

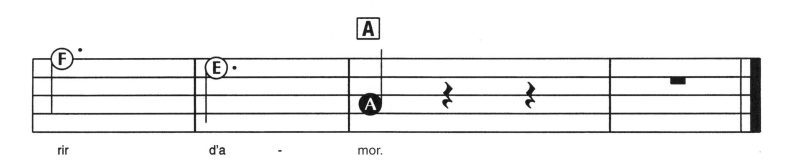

Toreador Song
from CARMEN

Registration 2
Rhythm: March

By Georges Bizet

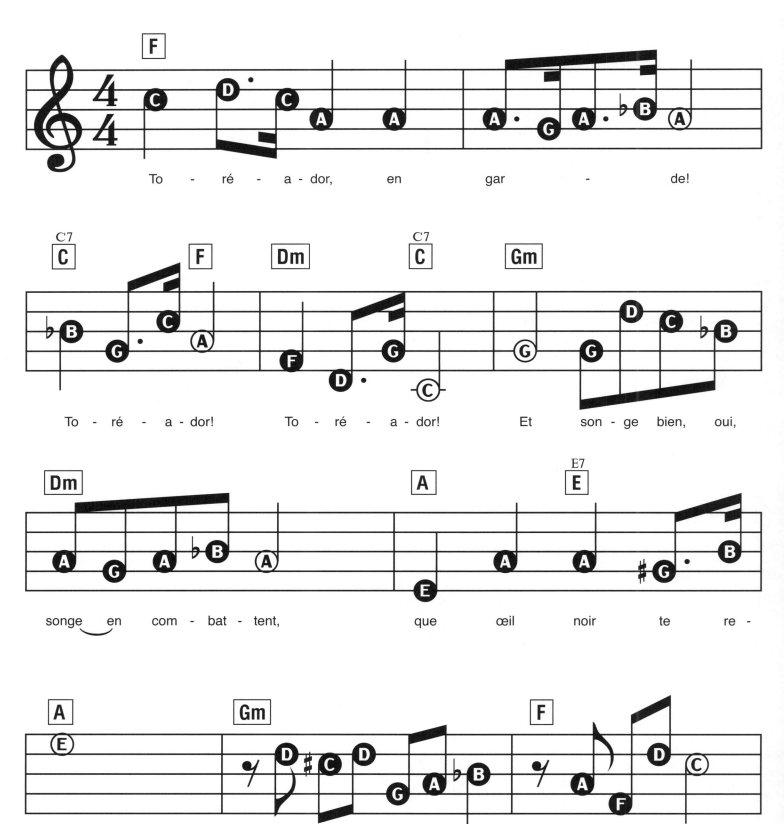

73

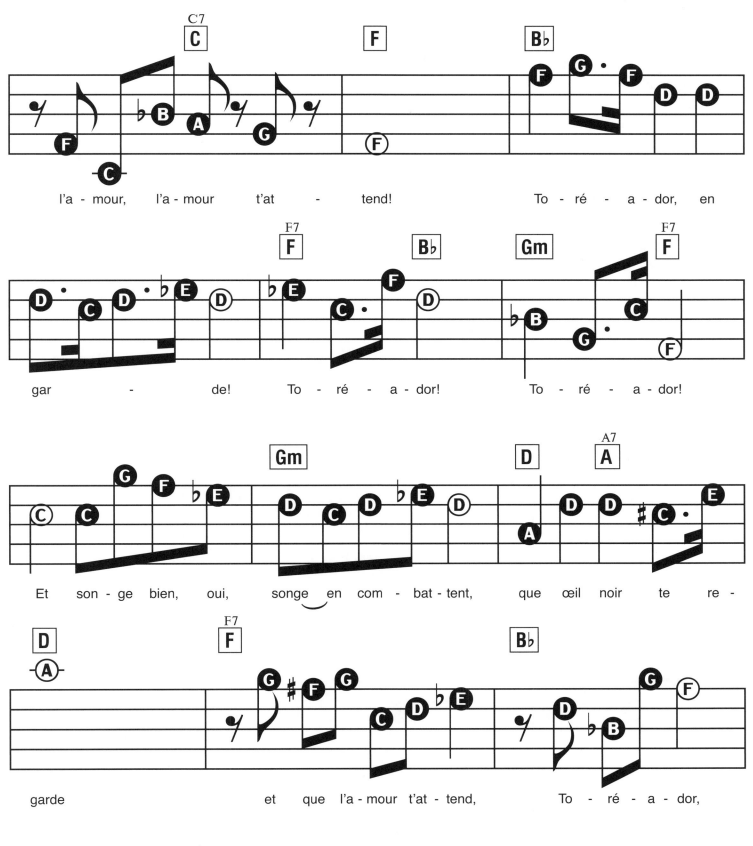

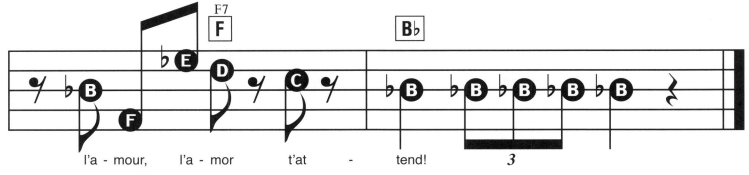

Triumphal March
from AIDA

Registration 2
Rhythm: March

By Giuseppe Verdi

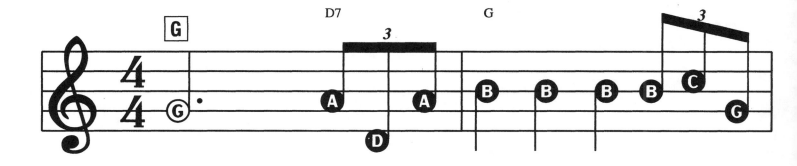

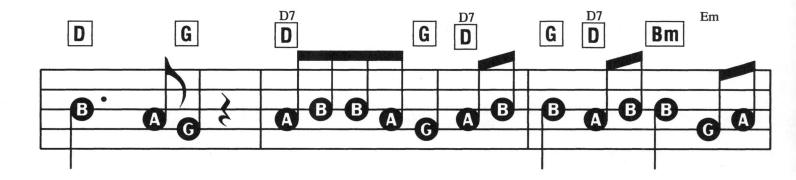

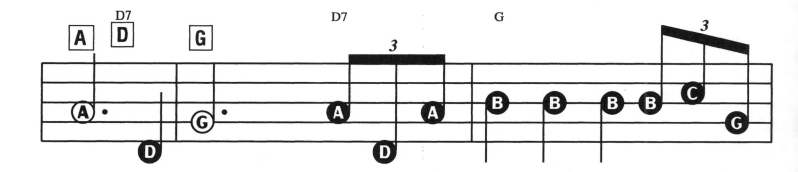

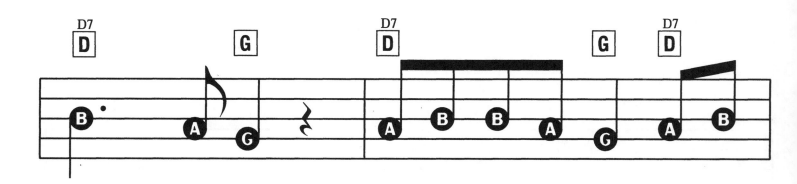

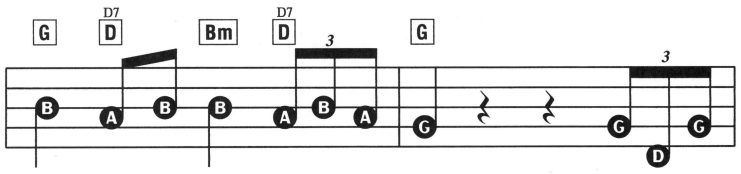

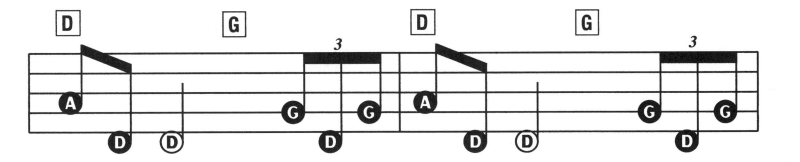

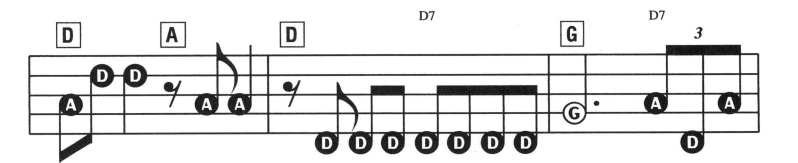

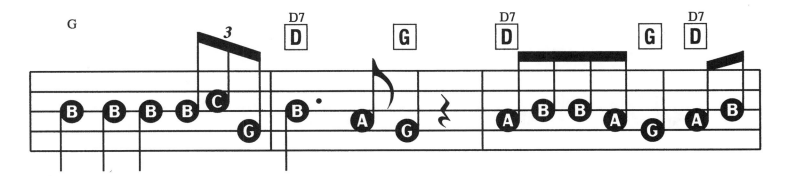

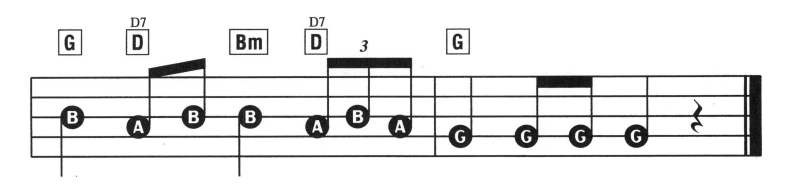

Un bel dì vedremo
from MADAMA BUTTERFLY

Registration 3
Rhythm: Waltz or None

By Giacomo Puccini

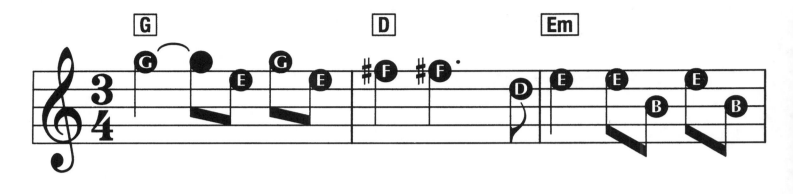

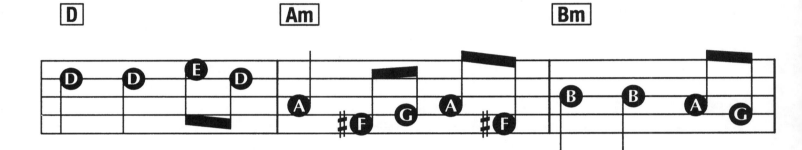

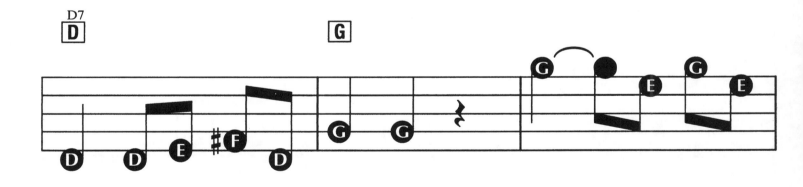

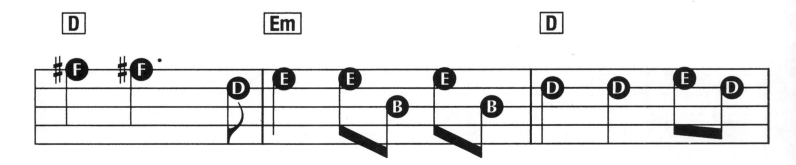

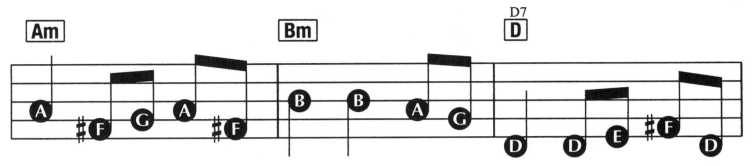

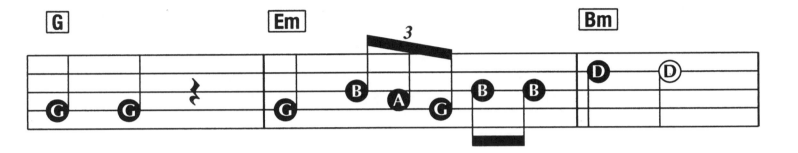

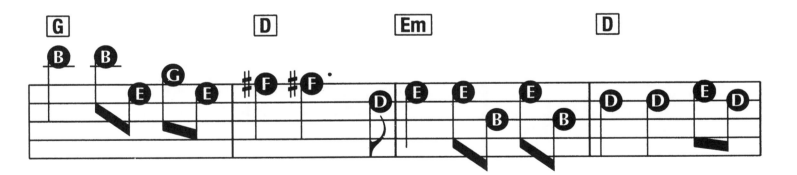

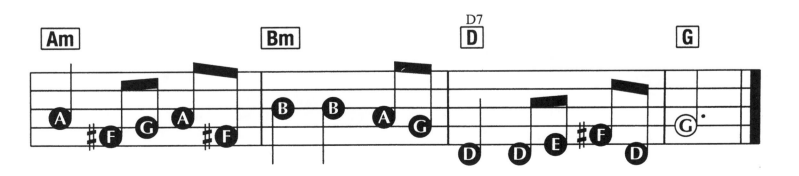

Vesti la giubba
from PAGLIACCI

Registration 3
Rhythm: Ballad

By Ruggero Leoncavallo

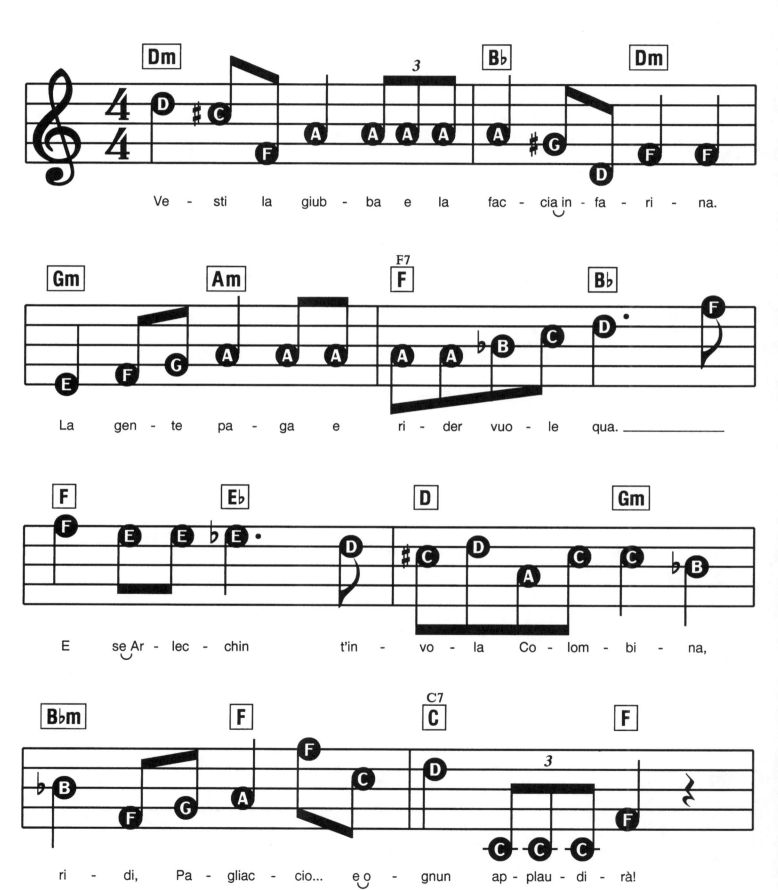

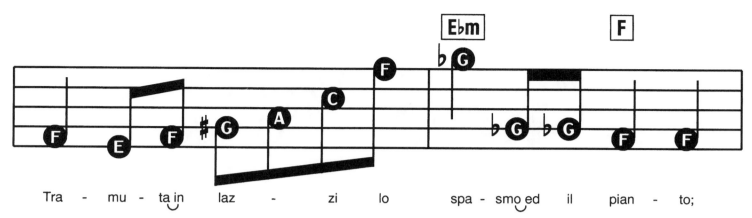

Tra - mu - ta in laz - zi lo spa - smo ed il pian - to;

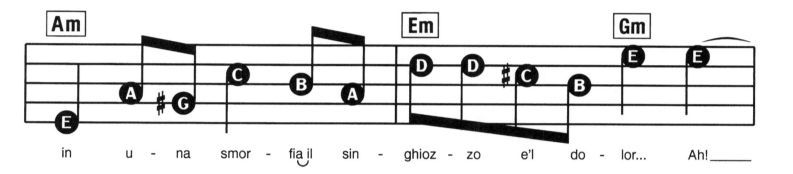

in u - na smor - fia il sin - ghioz - zo e'l do - lor... Ah!_____

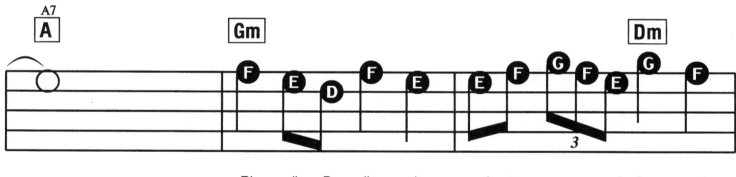

_____ Ri - di, Pa - gliac - cio, sul tuo a - mo-re in fran - to!

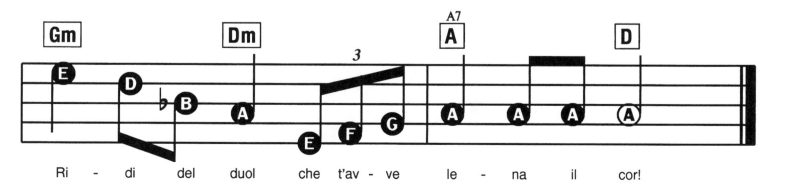

Ri - di del duol che t'av - ve - le - na il cor!

Registration Guide

• Match the Registration number on the song to the corresponding numbered category below. Select and activate an instrumental sound available on your instrument.

• Choose an automatic rhythm appropriate to the mood and style of the song. (Consult your Owner's Guide for proper operation of automatic rhythm features.)

• Adjust the tempo and volume controls to comfortable settings.

Registration

1	Mellow	Flutes, Clarinet, Oboe, Flugel Horn, Trombone, French Horn, Organ Flutes
2	Ensemble	Brass Section, Sax Section, Wind Ensemble, Full Organ, Theater Organ
3	Strings	Violin, Viola, Cello, Fiddle, String Ensemble, Pizzicato, Organ Strings
4	Guitars	Acoustic/Electric Guitars, Banjo, Mandolin, Dulcimer, Ukulele, Hawaiian Guitar
5	Mallets	Vibraphone, Marimba, Xylophone, Steel Drums, Bells, Celesta, Chimes
6	Liturgical	Pipe Organ, Hand Bells, Vocal Ensemble, Choir, Organ Flutes
7	Bright	Saxophones, Trumpet, Mute Trumpet, Synth Leads, Jazz/Gospel Organs
8	Piano	Piano, Electric Piano, Honky Tonk Piano, Harpsichord, Clavi
9	Novelty	Melodic Percussion, Wah Trumpet, Synth, Whistle, Kazoo, Perc. Organ
10	Bellows	Accordion, French Accordion, Mussette, Harmonica, Pump Organ, Bagpipes